The art

MW01600114

A book about appreciating and positively shaping solitude, personal freedom, and self-discovery.

Chapter overview

1. Introduction: Why being alone is important

1.1 The meaning of being alone in a networked world

In an increasingly connected world, where constant accessibility and digital connections are ubiquitous, being alone takes on a special significance. Amid the constant stream of information, news and social interactions, it is crucial to consciously seek and appreciate moments of seclusion and solitude.

Being alone offers a valuable opportunity to calm down, regenerate and sort out one's thoughts. It allows us to distance ourselves from outside influences and focus on our inner selves. By taking time to get to know ourselves better, we can see our needs, desires and goals more clearly and establish a deeper connection with ourselves.

In addition, being alone opens up the possibility of personal freedom for us. It frees us from social expectations and norms, allows us to define our own identity independently of others, and encourages us to pursue our passions and interests without having to compromise.

In a connected world where constant communication and social interaction are encouraged, being alone can be seen as taboo or have negative connotations. But it is important to realize that being alone does not mean loneliness at all. Rather, it is a conscious decision to spend time with oneself in order to find inner balance and build personal strength.

By recognizing and valuing the importance of being alone in a connected world, we can develop a positive attitude towards our own society. It enables us to be more aware of our lives, to use our inner resources, and to advance our self-discovery. Being alone can become a source of inspiration, creativity and self-realization, helping us to live a fulfilled and authentic life.

1.2 Social prejudices and misconceptions about loneliness

Loneliness is often negatively evaluated in our society and associated with stigmatization and pity. There are many prejudices and misconceptions about loneliness that need to be overcome in order to develop a more comprehensive understanding of this topic. A common prejudice is that loneliness is a sign of weakness or failure. People who are alone are often mistakenly viewed as unsociable, uninteresting, or unhappy. These prejudices can lead to social pressures that cause people to avoid or hide loneliness. Another misconception is to equate loneliness exclusively with social isolation. It is important to understand that loneliness does not necessarily mean a lack of relationships or social interaction. Someone can feel lonely despite having a large circle of friends or family if emotional connection is lacking or relationships are superficial.

In addition, loneliness is often viewed as a personal failure rather than a natural experience that everyone goes through to some degree. In a society that values success, productivity and constant activity, being alone is often seen as a waste of time and can be associated with shame.

It is important to challenge these preconceptions and misconceptions and promote a more nuanced understanding of loneliness. Loneliness is a multifaceted emotion that is influenced by many factors, such as personal circumstances, life stages, or individual preferences. It can also have positive aspects, such as the opportunity for self-reflection, strengthening inner bonds, and personal development.

By overcoming these societal prejudices and misconceptions about loneliness, we can create a supportive environment that enables people to acknowledge their own loneliness and find constructive ways to manage it. Dealing with loneliness in an open and respectful way can help people feel less isolated and find support in creating fulfilling and valuable alone time.

1.3 The positive aspects of being alone and why it is worth discovering them

Being alone holds a variety of positive aspects that make it worthwhile to explore and appreciate. By consciously taking time for ourselves and engaging in being alone, we can gain a number of valuable experiences and benefit from the following advantages:

Self-reflection and self-development: Being alone allows us to calmly deal with our own thoughts and get to know ourselves better. Self-reflection allows us to see our values, goals and needs more clearly and to develop our personality. It opens up the possibility of strengthening our self-confidence and gaining a deeper understanding of ourselves.

Creative freedom and personal development: When we are alone, we have the freedom to shape our time and energy according to our own ideas and interests. We can focus entirely on our creative inclinations, hobbies and passions without having to compromise. Being alone gives us the space to express our creativity and focus on personal projects and goals.

Inner strength and resilience: Being alone can help us build inner strength and develop resilience. By overcoming challenges and difficulties in moments of solitude, we learn to trust ourselves and manage our own resources. It strengthens our stamina and our ability to motivate ourselves and remain steadfast even in difficult times.

Rediscovering hobbies and our own interests: Often our own hobbies and interests get short shrift in our hectic daily lives and social obligations. Being alone gives us the opportunity to reconnect with our passions and experience them more intensely. We can immerse ourselves in our favorite activities, develop new skills, and push ourselves forward in our personal growth.

By recognizing and appreciating the positive aspects of being alone, we can lead fulfilling and enriching lives. Being alone offers us space for self-development, creativity and personal growth. It allows us to connect more deeply with ourselves and strengthen our individual identity. By consciously creating alone time, we can enrich our lives and find a balance between social interaction and personal freedom.

1.3.1 Self-reflection and self-development

One of the most significant positive aspects of being alone is the opportunity for self-reflection and self-development. When we consciously take time for ourselves, we can create a space to explore our thoughts, feelings, and experiences. Here are some important aspects of self-reflection and self-development in the context of being alone:

Exploration of one's inner self: Being alone allows us to distance ourselves from external distractions and focus on our inner world. We can explore our thoughts and emotions, question our values and beliefs, and develop a deeper understanding of ourselves. This allows us to more clearly define our identity and personal goals.

Clarification of our own needs and desires: Often in everyday life we are shaped by the expectations of other people or social norms. Being alone offers us the space to identify and understand our own needs and desires. By taking time to explore our innermost desires, we can make more conscious choices and live a life that matches our individual values and priorities.

Personal growth and self-improvement: Being alone allows us to work on ourselves and grow personally. By honestly facing our strengths and weaknesses, we can work on ourselves specifically and develop further. We can learn new skills, step out of our comfort zone and take on new challenges. This process of personal growth can lead to increased self-confidence and self-efficacy.

Self-care and self-love: Being alone opens up the possibility of meeting ourselves with loving attention and taking care of our own well-being. We can make time for activities that bring us joy, such as relaxation techniques, meditation, physical exercise, or reading inspirational books. By taking care of ourselves and treating ourselves with self-love, we can strengthen our inner balance and contentment.

Through the practice of self-reflection and self-development in solitude, we can continuously evolve, develop our own potential, and build a deeper connection with ourselves. It enables us to make more conscious choices, shape our direction in life, and live a more fulfilling and authentic life. Being alone thus becomes a valuable tool for personal growth and self-development.

1.3.2 Creative freedom and personal development

Being alone offers us a unique opportunity for creative freedom and personal development. Spending time in solitude opens up various opportunities to explore our creative side and develop our personality. Here are some important aspects of creative freedom and personal development in the context of being alone:

Independence from external influences: In moments of solitude, we can detach ourselves from the expectations and opinions of others and freely develop our creative vision. We have the freedom to explore our own interests, passions and talents without having to conform or compromise. This opens up new ways for us to express our creativity and pursue our personal goals.

Deepening hobbies and interests: Being alone gives us the opportunity to engage more deeply with our hobbies and interests. We can delve into our favorite activities, develop new skills, and evolve our passions. By devoting ourselves to our creative expressions, we can gain a deeper understanding of ourselves and discover a source of joy and fulfillment.

Experimentation and risk-taking: When we are alone, we often feel freer to try out new ideas and take risks. We can explore unconventional approaches, let our intuition guide us, and think outside the box. Being alone encourages us to expand our creative horizons and explore new directions without the limitations or judgments of others.

Self-expression and authenticity: Being alone allows us to express ourselves authentically without having to compromise. We can explore our own ideas, opinions and emotions and develop our personal style. Through creative self-expression in solitude, we can strengthen our individuality and connect more deeply with our inner truth.

The creative freedom and personal development in solitude allow us to fire our imagination, discover new paths and develop our artistic side. It is a time of creative flow where we can be inspired, expand our boundaries and express our personality. Being alone thus becomes fertile ground for our creative unfolding and personal development.

1.3.3 Inner strength and resilience

Being alone offers us the opportunity to build inner strength and develop resilience. It enables us to face challenges, deal with difficulties and strengthen our resilience. Here are some important aspects of inner strength and resilience in the context of being alone:

Self-confidence and independence: When we are alone, we are on our own and must act on our own responsibility. This promotes the development of self-confidence and independence. We learn to rely on our own abilities, make decisions and stand up for ourselves. Being on our own enables us to recognize our inner strength and acknowledge our own value.

Dealing with loneliness and isolation: Being alone can be accompanied by loneliness and isolation. It challenges us to deal with these feelings and find ways to manage them. By confronting our own emotions and developing strategies for self-care, we strengthen our psychological resilience. We learn how to comfort ourselves, use positive resources, and bounce back from difficult times.

Seeing challenges as opportunities for growth: Being alone can present us with various challenges. It requires us to motivate ourselves to leave our comfort zone and experience new things. By viewing these challenges as opportunities for growth, we can strengthen our inner strength and resilience. We learn to learn from setbacks, adapt and emerge stronger from difficult situations.

Self-care and self-compassion: In solitude, we have the opportunity to take care of ourselves and treat ourselves with compassion. We can take time for self-care, identify our needs, and do good for ourselves. By treating ourselves with kindness and compassion, we strengthen our inner resilience and develop a healthy relationship with ourselves.

Being alone thus becomes a way to build inner strength and resilience. By facing challenges, dealing with loneliness, and taking care of our own well-being, we develop mental resilience that enables us to remain steadfast and actively shape our lives even in difficult times.

1.3.4 Rediscovering hobbies and own interests

Being alone offers us a unique opportunity to connect with and rediscover our hobbies and our own interests. Often, these passions get short shrift in the hustle and bustle of everyday life and social obligations. Here are some important aspects of rediscovering hobbies and your own interests in the context of being alone:

Time and space for immersion: When we are alone, we have the opportunity to immerse ourselves in our hobbies and interests, without distractions or interruptions. We can focus entirely on the activities we enjoy and are absorbed in. Being alone allows us to improve our skills, learn new techniques, and develop our passions.

Creative Self-Expression: Being alone opens up the freedom to find and live out our own creative expression. We can immerse ourselves in various artistic mediums such as painting, writing, music, or crafts. By unleashing our creativity, we can express our personality, express ourselves, and find our individual voice.

Relaxation and relief: Our hobbies can provide us with valuable downtime and help us unwind. Being alone gives us the opportunity to unwind from stressful situations and focus on what we enjoy. Whether it's gardening, reading, cooking or other activities, our hobbies can help us relieve stress, calm the senses and reconnect with ourselves.

Self-development and personal growth: By rediscovering hobbies and our own interests, we can develop personally. We can learn new skills, try out areas that interest us, and develop our potential. Being on our own allows us to challenge ourselves, push our limits, and develop in our passions.

Being alone opens up the possibility of rediscovering our hobbies and interests and giving them a central role in our lives. By consciously making time for them, we can strengthen our passions, realize ourselves and lead a more fulfilling life. Alone time thus becomes a valuable tool for connecting with our innermost interests and fostering our personal development.

2. Understanding Loneliness: The Psychology of Loneliness

2.1 The distinction between loneliness and being alone

It is important to distinguish between loneliness and being alone, as these two terms have different meanings and implications. They are often mistakenly used interchangeably. Here are some important distinctions between loneliness and aloneness:

Loneliness: Loneliness refers to the negative feeling of feeling isolated, abandoned, or disconnected. It is a subjective sense of social deprivation and lack of emotional connection with other people. Loneliness can occur regardless of the presence or absence of other people and is often associated with negative emotions such as sadness, frustration, or anxiety.

Aloneness: Aloneness, on the other hand, refers to the state of being physically alone, without other people in close proximity. It is an objective situation in which one spends time without company. Being alone can involve both positive and negative experiences and is not necessarily associated with loneliness. It provides space for personal growth, self-reflection and creative expression.

Voluntariness: Another distinguishing feature is the voluntariness of the situation. Being alone can be consciously chosen in order to have time for oneself, while loneliness is often perceived as unwanted. When we consciously choose to be alone, we can use it as a positive experience to connect with ourselves and enhance our personal development.

Quality of Connection: Loneliness refers to the lack of deep emotional connection with others, while being alone provides the opportunity to connect more deeply with oneself. Being alone allows us to take time to get to know ourselves better, to explore our thoughts and feelings, and to understand our own needs and desires.

It is important that we realize that being alone in itself does not necessarily lead to loneliness. It can be a valuable time of self-reflection, personal growth, and creative expression. By understanding the distinction between solitude and being alone, we can appreciate and consciously use the positive aspects of being alone to empower ourselves and build a positive relationship with ourselves.

2.2 The different types of loneliness and their effects on well-being

Loneliness can come in different forms and have different effects on well-being. It is important to recognize these different types of loneliness in order to respond appropriately. Here are some of the most common forms of loneliness and their effects:

2.2.1 Emotional loneliness

Emotional loneliness refers to the feeling of lack of close emotional connections with others. It is the feeling that we do not feel understood, supported, or emotionally connected even when we are surrounded by others. Here are some important aspects of emotional loneliness and its effects:

Feeling isolated: People who suffer from emotional loneliness can feel isolated and alone, even when surrounded by other people. There can be a feeling that no one really understands what you are going through and that there is no one to confide in. This isolation can lead to feelings of alienation and disconnection from others.

Lack of support: Emotional loneliness can increase the feeling that there is no one to support us during difficult times. We may lack a trusted friend or family member with whom to share our concerns.

The lack of supportive social support can lead to feelings of being overwhelmed and helpless.

Effects on psychological well-being: Emotional loneliness can have a negative impact on mental well-being. People who feel emotionally lonely are at increased risk for depression, anxiety, and other mental illnesses. The prolonged absence of emotional connection can lead to feelings of sadness, emptiness, and frustration.

Need for emotional closeness: The need for emotional closeness and connection is fundamental to human well-being. When this need is not met, it can lead to a strong desire for emotional connection and a sense of longing. People who suffer from emotional loneliness may long to connect more deeply with others and to have their emotional needs met.

It is important that people suffering from emotional loneliness take their feelings seriously and take appropriate steps to cope. This may include building closer relationships with trusted people, participating in support groups, or seeking professional help. By connecting emotionally with others and attending to our own emotional needs, we can overcome emotional loneliness and improve our psychological well-being.

2.2.2 Social loneliness

Social loneliness refers to the feeling of lack of sufficient social contacts and a supportive social network. It is the feeling that we do not have enough social interactions or relationships to give us a sense of connection and belonging. Here are some important aspects of social loneliness and its effects:

Feeling isolated: People who suffer from social loneliness may feel isolated and cut off from others. They may feel that they are unable to make real connections or be accepted in social situations. This isolation can lead to feelings of limitation and lack of support.

Lack of social support: social loneliness can increase feelings of not having adequate social support. The lack of trusted friends, family members, or communities to provide support can lead to feelings of being overwhelmed and lacking support during difficult times.

Effects on psychological well-being: Social loneliness can have a negative impact on mental well-being. People who feel socially lonely are at increased risk for depression, anxiety, and other mental health problems. Feeling a lack of social connection can lead to feelings of emptiness, sadness, and frustration.

Desire for social interaction: The need for social interaction and belonging is fundamental to human well-being. When this need is not met, it can lead to a strong desire for social connection and a sense of missing. People who suffer from social loneliness may long to be included in relationships and social communities.

It is important that people suffering from social loneliness take steps to strengthen their social connections. This may include building new friendships, participating in social activities, or seeking out support groups. It can also be helpful to look for opportunities to support others and engage in community projects or volunteer activities. By feeling socially connected and being part of a supportive community, we can overcome social loneliness and improve our well-being.

2.2.3 Existential loneliness

Existential loneliness refers to the profound feeling of isolation or separation at an existential level. It is the feeling that no one really understands who we are, what we are going through, or the meaning of our lives. Here are some important aspects of existential loneliness and its effects:

Separation from others: Existential loneliness arises from a sense of separation from others at a deeper level. There can be a sense that our innermost experiences and thoughts cannot be shared or understood by others. This can lead to a sense of isolation and separation from the world.

Existential questions: Existential loneliness is often accompanied by questions about the meaning of life, one's own existence, and the meaning of being. People suffering from existential loneliness may be preoccupied with existential questions that cause them to question their own beliefs, values, and goals. This can lead to a feeling of lostness and insecurity.

Search for spiritual fulfillment: Existential loneliness can intensify the desire for spiritual or philosophical fulfillment. People may seek a deep connection with something greater, whether through religion, spirituality, or other philosophical beliefs. This can help answer existential questions and find deeper meaning in life.

Meaning and significance: Existential loneliness can reinforce the sense that our lives have no clear meaning or purpose. It can lead to a sense of emptiness and meaninglessness when we feel that our individual existence has no greater significance. This can lead to a search for meaning or purpose in life.

It is important for people suffering from existential loneliness to address these existential questions and find ways to support their search for meaning and significance. This may include reflecting on personal values and beliefs, learning techniques for self-reflection, and finding paths to spiritual or philosophical fulfillment. By addressing our existential questions and finding deeper meaning in our lives, we can overcome existential loneliness and move toward a deeper sense of connection and fulfillment.

2.2.4 Situational loneliness

Situational loneliness refers to the temporary or intermittent feeling of isolation due to specific life circumstances or situations. It is the feeling of being alone or not having enough social interactions that occurs in specific situations. Here are some important aspects of situational loneliness and its effects:

Geographic separation: Situational loneliness can occur when people are geographically separated from their social support networks. This can be caused by moving to a new city, losing friends or family members, or traveling for work. Feeling far away from familiar relationships can lead to temporary loneliness.

Life stages and changes: Situational loneliness may be associated with certain life stages or changes, such as transitioning into retirement, ending a relationship, leaving home, or entering adulthood. At such times, people may feel alone and insecure as they adjust to new situations and roles.

Illness or Injury: Situational loneliness can also occur because of illness or injury. When people are isolated due to health problems or physical limitations, they may feel they lack social interaction and support. This can lead to a temporary reduction in their social activities.

Work-related loneliness: Another aspect of situational loneliness relates to the work situation. People who work in isolated work environments or in jobs that allow little social interaction may feel lonely during their work hours. This can lead to a lack of social support and a sense of disconnection from colleagues.

It is important to understand that situational loneliness is often temporary and may be associated with specific circumstances. However, the impact on well-being and mental health can be noticeable. To manage situational loneliness, it is helpful to build social support systems, seek out social activities, join new communities, or otherwise connect with others. By attending to our social needs and intentionally connecting with others, we can overcome situational loneliness and strengthen our sense of connectedness.

2.3 The psychological factors that can lead to loneliness

Loneliness can be influenced by a variety of psychological factors. Here are some important psychological factors that can lead to loneliness:

Low self-esteem: People with low self-esteem tend to see themselves as less lovable or valuable. This can lead them to believe that other people reject them or are not interested in their company, which can lead to loneliness.

Social Anxiety: People with social anxiety often have difficulty feeling comfortable in social situations and building relationships. Fear of negative evaluation or rejection may cause them to avoid social interactions and feel isolated.

Perfectionism: Perfectionistic tendencies can contribute to feelings of loneliness. Perfectionists often set unrealistically high standards for themselves and for others. When these standards are not met, this can lead to feelings of disappointment and isolation.

Negative thinking patterns: Negative thinking patterns, such as pessimistic thinking or a tendency to make negative interpretations of social situations, can contribute to loneliness. When people tend to perceive social interactions as dismissive or unpleasant, this can lead to withdrawal from social relationships.

Lack of social skills: A lack of social skill development can cause people to have difficulty forming and maintaining close relationships. Lack of skills in handling social situations and difficulty reaching out to others can lead to loneliness.

Life events and losses: certain life events, such as the loss of a loved one, the end of a relationship, or a move to a new place, can lead to loneliness. These events can lead to a sense of loss of social support and connection.

It is important to recognize these psychological factors and understand how they can contribute to loneliness. By working on our self-esteem, managing social anxiety, developing more realistic thinking patterns, improving our social skills, and dealing with change and loss, we can reduce our loneliness and experience a more fulfilling social connection.

2.4 The importance of social interaction and relationships for a fulfilling life

Social interaction and relationships play a crucial role in a fulfilling life. Here are some important aspects that underline their importance:

Emotional support: Social interactions and relationships provide us with emotional support. Sharing feelings, concerns, and joys with others allows us to feel understood, supported, and loved. Emotional support from others helps us reduce stress, strengthen our mental health, and maintain a positive outlook on life.

Sharing experiences: Social interaction allows us to share our experiences with others. Sharing successes, challenges, and everyday experiences with others allows us to connect with each other and broaden our perspectives. It also allows us to learn from the experiences of others and gain new insights.

Support in difficult times: Social relationships provide vital support during difficult times. When we face challenges, grief, or loss, we can rely on our relationships to carry us through these times. The emotional support and practical help from others can help us feel stronger and less alone.

Social Identity and Belonging: Social interactions and relationships contribute to the development of our social identity. Through our relationships, we define ourselves, find our place in society, and feel we belong. Social connections provide us with opportunities to identify with others and share common values, interests, and goals.

Meaningful Relationships: Meaningful relationships give our lives deeper meaning and purpose. When we connect with others in meaningful and fulfilling ways, we can experience a sense of meaning and fulfillment. These relationships give us the opportunity to grow, learn and develop our full potential together.

It is important to actively maintain and strengthen social interactions and relationships. This can be done by building new relationships, maintaining existing friendships, participating in social activities, and developing social skills. By intentionally investing in our social relationships, we can live fulfilling lives characterized by connectedness, support, and meaningful encounters.

2.4.1 Emotional support

Emotional support is an essential component of social interaction and relationships. It refers to the availability of compassion, comfort, encouragement, and understanding from others. Here are some important aspects of emotional support:

Empathy and understanding: Through empathic listening and understanding, caregivers are able to understand our emotions and feelings. They take time to listen to us, give us space to express and reflect, and understand our perspectives. Feeling understood allows us to feel less alone and isolated.

Comfort and encouragement: Emotional support includes comfort and encouragement during difficult times. When we face challenges, loss, or disappointment, caregivers can comfort us and encourage us to keep going. Their words of support give us strength and confidence to deal with life's challenges.

Collaborative sharing of feelings: Emotional support involves sharing feelings together. By sharing our emotional experiences with others, we can feel connected and recognize that our feelings are not unique or unusual. This shared exchange creates an atmosphere of trust and openness in which we can feel safe to express our emotions.

Strengthening self-esteem: Emotional support can also help strengthen our self-esteem. When other people encourage us to believe in ourselves, acknowledge our strengths, and celebrate our successes, we feel valuable and valued. This positive reinforcement helps us maintain a healthy self-image and feel more confident.

Long-term relationships: Emotional support is often provided through long-term relationships and close ties. Family, friends, partners, or supportive communities can provide us with ongoing emotional support. These long-term relationships provide us with the security and confidence that we can count on support during difficult times.

Emotional support is critical to our well-being and mental health. It is important to recognize our needs for emotional support and actively work to build and maintain supportive relationships. By providing emotional support to each other and being there for others, we can create a supportive social network to assist us in all areas of life.

2.4.2 Sharing experiences

Sharing experiences with others plays a significant role in social interactions and relationships. Here are some important aspects of sharing experiences:

Connection and community: By sharing our experiences with others, we can experience a deep connection and sense of community. We realize that we are not alone in our experiences and that others are experiencing similar challenges, joys, or successes. Sharing experiences creates an atmosphere of cohesion and support.

Shifting perspectives: Sharing experiences allows us to take different perspectives and broaden our own views. By listening to the stories and experiences of others, we can gain new insights, reduce prejudices, and develop a deeper understanding of the diversity of human experience.

Learning and growth: By sharing experiences, we can learn from each other and develop personally. By sharing our experiences with others, we can benefit from their insights, advice and approaches. Mutual learning and sharing of knowledge promotes our personal growth and development.

Support and encouragement: Sharing experiences allows us to receive support and encouragement from others. When we go through challenges or difficulties, we can draw on the experiences and advice of others. They can encourage us to push through, find solutions, and try new ways of doing things.

Authentic relationships: Sharing experiences allows us to build authentic relationships. By sharing our true thoughts, feelings and experiences with others, we connect on a deeper level. This allows us to get to know each other better, build trust, and create relationships of meaning and depth.

Sharing experiences requires openness, honesty, and a willingness to be vulnerable. By sharing our stories and listening to others, we can support, inspire, and grow together. Sharing experiences allows us to live richer and more fulfilling social lives.

2.4.3 Support in difficult times

Social interactions and relationships provide us with important support during difficult times. Here are some aspects of support we can receive from others:

Emotional support: During difficult times, relationships can provide us with emotional support. The compassion, encouragement, and comforting words of others can help us cope with our emotional burdens. They can make us feel that we are not alone and that our feelings and reactions are normal.

Practical help: In some situations, we need practical help to cope with challenges. Family, friends, or other supportive people can be at our side during such times. They can support us with everyday tasks, take the pressure off us and help us take the necessary steps to overcome a difficult situation.

Advice and perspective: Often other people can help us with their advice and perspective when we are faced with decisions or problems. They can give us new insights, show us alternative solutions, and help us make wise decisions. Advice from trusted people can help us better manage our situation.

A safe environment: In difficult times, it is important to have a safe and supportive environment. Relationships can provide such a space for us to express ourselves freely and share our concerns and fears without being judged or devalued. Such an environment allows us to open up and receive support without the fear of rejection.

Long-term support: In difficult times, we often need continuous support. Relationships built over a long period of time can provide us with this ongoing support. The trust and reliability of such relationships enable us to lean on them and rely on their support.

It is important to ask for support and accept help in difficult times. We should be aware that it is normal and healthy to accept support from others and that this does not make us weak. By taking advantage of the support that is available to us, we can better navigate through difficult times and emerge stronger.

2.4.4 Social identity and affiliation

Social identity and belonging play a critical role in our well-being and mental health. Here are some aspects of the importance of social identity and belonging:

Self-definition and self-esteem: Our social identity is closely linked to our self-esteem. Belonging to certain groups or communities allows us to define ourselves and develop a positive self-perception. By being part of a social group, we feel recognized, valued and valuable.

Support and networks: Belonging to social groups provides us with a supportive network. We have people around us with whom we feel connected, who support us and with whom we can exchange ideas. These networks can help us overcome challenges, share resources, and stand by us during difficult times.

Shared values and interests: By belonging to social groups, we find people who share similar values, interests and goals. This allows us to be in an environment that matches our beliefs and interests. We can inspire and motivate each other and support each other in our personal development.

Identity affirmation: Belonging to social groups provides us with the opportunity to affirm our identity. By identifying with others who have similar characteristics, experiences, or backgrounds, we feel understood and accepted. This affirmation of our identity strengthens our self-confidence and our sense of well-being.

Integration and social togetherness: Belonging to social groups enables us to integrate into society and experience a sense of social togetherness. This sense of belonging creates a sense of connection and commitment to common goals. It helps strengthen the social fabric and promotes the overall well-being of a community.

Recognizing our social identity and seeking to belong are natural human needs. By engaging in social groups and becoming part of communities, we can experience a sense of connection, understanding and support. This strengthens our well-being and contributes to a fulfilling life.

2.4.5 Meaningful relationships

Meaningful relationships are of particular importance for our well-being and life satisfaction. Here are some aspects of the importance of meaningful relationships:

Meaning and Purpose: Meaningful relationships give our lives meaning and purpose. They allow us to connect with others, share common values and goals, and commit ourselves to something greater than ourselves. These relationships give us a sense that our lives have meaning and that we are part of something significant.

Growth and development: Meaningful relationships promote our personal growth and development. By sharing ideas, experiences and resources with others, we can inspire, support and encourage each other. These relationships provide a platform for us to develop, learn new skills, and realize our potential.

Support in difficult times: Meaningful relationships are a source of support when we face challenges. In difficult times, we can rely on our closest relationships to provide us with emotional support, practical help and comfort. They make us feel that we are not alone and that together we can overcome obstacles.

Shared joy and successes: Meaningful relationships enable us to share joy and successes with others. When we share our triumphs, accomplishments and happy moments with people we care about, it enhances our happiness and satisfaction. Joy becomes more intense when shared with others, and it creates a deep connection between people.

Long-term bonds: Meaningful relationships are often characterized by long-term bonds. Strong connections are formed through shared history, shared experiences, and growth over time. These relationships provide continuity, stability and reliability, which gives us a sense of security and belonging.

Meaningful relationships require investment and nurturing. They require time, attention, empathy and the will to support and nurture each other. By focusing on and actively cultivating meaningful relationships, we can lead fulfilling and meaningful lives. These relationships enrich us on many levels and contribute to our personal growth, satisfaction and well-being.

3.

3. the advantages of being alone: the positive side of loneliness

3.1 The opportunity for self-reflection and self-development

The art of being alone allows us valuable time for self-reflection and self-development. Here are some aspects of how we can take advantage of these opportunities:

Inner mindfulness: Being alone creates space for inner mindfulness. By consciously taking time to get in touch with ourselves, we can better understand our thoughts, feelings and needs. We can hear our inner voice and learn to trust our intuition. Inner mindfulness helps us to reflect and align our values, goals and life priorities.

Self-exploration: Being alone gives us the opportunity to explore and discover ourselves. We can explore our interests, talents and passions. We can try new hobbies, discover creative forms of expression, or rethink our personal goals and dreams. Self-exploration allows us to get to know ourselves better and strengthen our individual identity.

Self-acceptance and self-compassion: Being alone gives us the chance to accept ourselves and be compassionate with ourselves.

We can accept our weaknesses and mistakes and forgive ourselves. Self-acceptance and self-compassion allow us to build a healthy self-esteem and be loving towards ourselves. This promotes our psychological well-being and inner strength.

Personal growth goals: Being alone opens up the space for us to define and pursue our personal growth goals. We can focus on our individual development and take deliberate steps to improve in the areas that are important to us. This may include personal growth, learning new skills, or overcoming fears and limitations. Personal growth promotes our self-development and potential.

Self-care and recreation: Being alone gives us the opportunity to take care of our own needs and well-being. We can take time for relaxation, recreation and self-care. This may include connecting with books, music or nature, practicing meditation or yoga, or engaging in other activities that bring us joy and recharge our energy.

Being alone offers us the precious chance to meet ourselves and focus on our personal development. It allows us to connect with our inner world and build a deeper connection with ourselves. By taking advantage of the opportunity for self-reflection and self-development, we can evolve, realize our goals and live a fulfilling life.

3.2 Creative freedom and personal development through solitude

Being alone opens up a world of creative freedom and personal development for us. Here are some aspects of how we can take advantage of these opportunities:

Self-expression: When we are alone, we have the freedom to express ourselves in our own way. We can express our thoughts, ideas, and emotions in creative ways, whether through writing, painting, music, dance, or other forms of artistic expression. Being alone creates a space where we can express ourselves freely, without restrictions or judgments from others.

Unconventional thinking: Being alone allows us to break free from societal norms and expectations and cultivate unconventional thinking. We have the freedom to develop our own ideas, explore new perspectives, and find innovative approaches to solving problems. The absence of outside influences allows us to open our minds and discover new ways of thinking.

Self-motivation and goal setting: Being alone gives us space to set our own goals and motivate ourselves. Without the influences or expectations of others, we can focus on what is truly important to us. We can challenge ourselves to push our limits and pursue our personal goals. This encourages our self-responsibility and strengthens our sense of accomplishment.

Experimentation and risk-taking: When we are alone, we can allow ourselves to experiment and take risks. We can try new things without worrying about the opinions or expectations of others. Being alone allows us to get to know ourselves better and step out of our comfort zone. By allowing ourselves to make mistakes and learn from them, we can grow and develop personally.

Self-actualization: Being alone opens up the possibility of self-actualization and of pursuing our own dreams and passions. It gives us the freedom to discover our own interests, pursue our passions and develop our individual abilities. By focusing on our personal development, we can live a fulfilling and authentic life.

Being alone offers us the chance to discover our creative side and enhance our personal development. It allows us to explore and live out our own unique talents and passions. By taking advantage of the creative freedom that being alone offers, we can express ourselves, explore new paths, and strengthen our creative identity.

3.3 The chance to build inner strength and resilience

Being alone offers us a valuable opportunity to build inner strength and resilience. Here are some aspects of how we can take advantage of these opportunities:

Self-reflection and self-awareness: Being alone allows us to take an intense look at ourselves. Through self-reflection and self-awareness, we get to know our strengths, weaknesses, values and needs better. This deep understanding of ourselves forms the basis for inner strength and resilience.

Self-care: Being alone gives us the opportunity to take care of our own needs intensively. We can strengthen our self-care practices, such as regular exercise, healthy eating, getting enough sleep, and managing stress. By taking care of ourselves, we strengthen our mental and physical health, which makes us more resilient in the face of challenges.

Emotional regulation: Being alone gives us space to explore our emotions and learn to regulate them in a healthy way. We can accept our feelings and thoughts, reflect on them, and learn to manage them. By developing our emotional skills, we are better able to deal with difficult situations and strengthen our resilience.

Self-confidence and self-empowerment: Being alone opens up the opportunity to build our self-confidence and self-empowerment. We can challenge ourselves to try new things and celebrate successes. By overcoming obstacles and achieving our goals, we gain self-confidence and develop a sense of self-efficacy, which makes us more resilient to life's challenges.

Acceptance of change and uncertainty: Being alone gives us the opportunity to deal with change and uncertainty. We learn that change is a natural part of life and that we can adapt and grow. By strengthening our ability to adapt and be flexible, we develop resilience and the ability to adapt to life's challenges.

Being alone offers us the opportunity to build inner strength and resilience that will help us deal with life's ups and downs. By focusing on ourselves, connecting with our inner resources and working on our personal development, we can strengthen our resilience and emerge stronger from difficult times.

3.4 The rediscovery of hobbies, passions and own interests

Being alone offers us the opportunity to rediscover and deepen our hobbies, passions and own interests. Here are some aspects of how we can take advantage of this opportunity:

Time for self-pleasure: In solitude, we have the freedom to focus entirely on our own interests and hobbies without having to consider others. We can take time to do the things that bring us joy and fulfill us. This can be reading a book, practicing a musical instrument, painting, writing, or any other activity that excites us.

Self-development and personal growth: By rediscovering and deepening our hobbies and interests, we can develop ourselves and grow personally. We can learn new skills, expand our knowledge, and develop in our chosen field. Devotion to our interests allows us to enhance our creative and intellectual abilities and enrich ourselves as individuals.

Flow Experiences: Being alone offers us the opportunity to immerse ourselves in a state of "flow." Flow refers to the state of being completely absorbed in an activity where we are challenged while using our skills. By focusing on our hobbies and interests, we can experience such flow experiences that give us a sense of fulfillment and satisfaction.

Self-expression and authenticity: Being alone allows us to pursue our own interests and express ourselves in an authentic way. We can express our creativity and develop our individual style. Living out our hobbies and interests allows us to get to know ourselves better and celebrate our uniqueness.

Relaxation and stress relief: Our hobbies and interests also serve as a valuable source of relaxation and stress relief. By immersing ourselves in activities we enjoy, we can leave everyday stress behind and find peace. This contributes to our mental and emotional well-being and helps us find a healthy balance in our lives.

Being alone opens up the opportunity to discover, nurture and enjoy our hobbies, passions and own interests. By taking time for our personal preferences, we strengthen our individual growth, self-expression and well-being. Rediscovering our hobbies and interests enriches our lives and adds an extra dimension of fulfillment.

4. Mastering loneliness: strategies for being fulfilled alone

4.1 Self-care and self-love as a basis

Self-care and self-love form the fundamental basis for a fulfilling life living alone. Here are some aspects of how we can use self-care and self-love as a foundation:

Acceptance and appreciation: Self-care begins with acceptance and appreciation of ourselves. We acknowledge that we are unique, with our strengths and weaknesses, our successes and failures. By accepting ourselves and valuing ourselves, we create a space of self-love.

Self-care: Self-care involves consciously taking care of our physical, emotional and mental well-being. We pay attention to our needs and take care of ourselves. This can mean getting enough rest, choosing healthy food, integrating regular exercise, and taking time for relaxation and balance.

Setting boundaries: Self-care includes setting and enforcing boundaries. We learn to say "no" when it is necessary for us to do so and to protect ourselves from excessive stress or exploitation. By respecting our boundaries, we show appreciation to ourselves and pay attention to our own needs and limits.

Self-reflection and mindfulness: Self-care involves the practice of self-reflection and mindfulness. We take time to listen within ourselves, to recognize and understand our feelings, thoughts, and needs. Through mindfulness, we learn to be present in the present moment and consciously care for ourselves.

Self-compassion: Self-care also involves cultivating self-compassion. We treat ourselves with kindness and understanding, as we would a loved one. By treating ourselves with compassion, we accept ourselves, even in difficult times, and create a space of loving care for ourselves.

The practice of self-care and self-love forms the foundation for a healthy and fulfilling life on our own. By taking care of ourselves, we create a solid foundation for our well-being and personal development. Consciously caring for our needs, setting boundaries, and lovingly accepting ourselves support us in living a fulfilling and authentic life while living alone.

4.2 The development of a positive attitude towards being alone

A positive attitude toward being alone can help to realize the benefits and opportunities of this time of self-reflection and personal growth. Here are some aspects of how we can develop a positive attitude towards being alone:

Acceptance of our own company: Instead of viewing being alone as negative or unpleasant, we can learn to appreciate and accept our own company. By consciously choosing to spend our time alone, we can focus on ourselves and build a deeper connection to our inner world.

Self-reflection and mindfulness: Being alone offers us space for self-reflection and mindfulness. By consciously taking time to listen within and recognize our thoughts, feelings and needs, we can better understand ourselves and grow. We can reflect on our personal goals, values and dreams and align our actions with them.

Seize opportunities for self-development: Being alone allows us to focus on our personal development. We can take on new challenges, develop skills, pursue creative projects, and pursue our passions. By taking advantage of these opportunities, we can lead fulfilling and meaningful lives, independent of the presence of others.

Enjoyment of our own interests and hobbies: Being alone gives us the opportunity to focus on our own interests and hobbies without having to consider others. We can pursue our passions, try new activities, and express our creativity. By using our time alone to engage in the things we enjoy, we can experience a deeper sense of fulfillment.

Self-love and self-care: A positive attitude towards being alone also includes self-love and self-care. By treating ourselves with kindness, compassion and acceptance, we create a positive relationship with ourselves. We pay attention to our own needs, care for ourselves, and look after our well-being. This strengthens our inner strength and resilience.

A positive attitude towards being alone enables us to view solitude as a valuable time of self-discovery and personal development. By consciously choosing to appreciate and take advantage of this time, we can live a fulfilling and meaningful life in solitude.

4.3 Practical tips for organizing alone time and dealing with feelings of loneliness

Alone time can be an enriching and transformative time, but it also requires intentional action to make it positive. Here are some practical tips for shaping alone time and dealing with feelings of loneliness:

4.3.1 Planning alone time

Consciously planning alone time is crucial to reaping the full benefits of being alone. Here are some practical steps for planning and creating your alone time:

Determine the time frame: Decide how much alone time you want to have. It can be a short break in your daily routine or a whole weekend where you retreat.

Create a suitable space: Find a quiet and pleasant space where you feel comfortable and can focus on yourself without being disturbed. This can be your home, a café, a park or another place that offers you peace and privacy.

Identify your interests and needs: Think about what activities inspire, delight, and fulfill you. Make a list of hobbies, books, movies, music, or other interests you want to explore during your alone time. Also consider your needs for rest, relaxation, or physical activity.

Set clear goals: Define clear goals for your alone time. Do you want to focus on self-reflection, try a new hobby, read a book, or just relax? By setting clear goals, you can use your alone time more effectively.

Create a supportive environment: Make sure you don't have any unnecessary distractions during your alone time. Put your cell phone on silent or set it aside, inform your roommates or family about your alone time and ask them for understanding and privacy.

Use time consciously: During your alone time, be mindful and focused on what you are doing. Avoid multitasking and don't get distracted by other tasks. Be fully present in the moment and enjoy the experience of being alone.

Flexibility and self-care: Be flexible in your planning and listen to your own needs. If you notice that you feel tired, rest. If you try a new activity and find you don't like it, be open to change and find something that suits you better.

Reflect after your alone time: After your alone time is over, take time to reflect. Think about what you learned during this time, what insights you gained, and how you can integrate these experiences into your everyday life.

Planning alone time allows you to be intentional with your time and make being alone a valuable time of self-discovery and personal growth. By following these steps, you can get the most out of your alone time and build a deeper connection with yourself.

4.3.2 Self-care routine

A regular self-care routine is essential to taking care of your physical, emotional, and mental well-being during alone time. Here are some practical steps to create your own self-care routine:

Prioritize self-care: Recognize the importance of self-care and make it a priority in your life. Understand that you must take care of yourself in order to live a healthy and fulfilling life.

Identify your needs: Take time to identify and understand your own needs. Ask yourself what gives you energy, what relaxes you and what makes you happy. Everyone has different needs, so it's important to identify your individual needs.

Create a list of self-care activities: Make a list of activities that bring you joy and recharge you. These can be activities like taking a warm bath, enjoying a cup of tea, practicing yoga, meditating, reading a book, taking a walk, or preparing a healthy meal. Write these activities down and keep them handy.

Schedule time for self-care: Consciously schedule time in your daily routine for self-care. Whether it's in the morning, evening or any other time doesn't matter. Find a time that works best for you and create a regular routine.

Stay consistent: Stick to your self-care routine and be consistent. Self-care should not be an occasional activity, but an integral part of your lifestyle. Commit to setting aside time for yourself on a regular basis.

Experiment and find what works: Be open to new self-care practices and experiment to find what works best for you. Everyone is unique, so it's important to find out what activities and routines bring you the most joy and relaxation.

Connect with your body: Pay attention to your body and its needs. Exercise regularly, eat a balanced diet, and get enough sleep. Good physical health is fundamental to your well-being.

Be mindful and present in the moment: When performing your self-care activities, be mindful and present in the present moment. Let go of your thoughts about the past or future and focus fully on what you are doing right now.

Creating a self-care routine allows you to support, recharge and be compassionate with yourself. By making time for self-care on a regular basis, you can boost your energy and resilience and live a balanced and fulfilling life.

4.3.3 Creative activities

Creative activities can be an enriching and fulfilling experience during alone time. They give you the opportunity to explore your artistic side, unleash your imagination, and express your emotions. Here are some ideas for creative activities you can try during your alone time:

Paint or draw: Pick up pens, brushes and paints and let your creative energy flow onto the canvas or paper. Paint abstract artworks, portraits or landscapes - there are no limits to your creativity.

Writing: Sit down and write in a journal, compose poems or short stories. Let your thoughts run free and express your emotions and thoughts on paper.

Crafts or tinkering: Explore craft activities such as knitting, sewing, pottery, modeling or origami. Create something with your own hands and enjoy the process of creating.

Make music: Play an instrument, sing, compose your own songs or listen to music that inspires you. Music can be a powerful form of expression and positively influence your mood.

Photography: Take your camera or smartphone and go on a journey of discovery. Take pictures of nature, interesting places or people. Let your creativity blossom by capturing unique moments.

Cook or bake: Use your alone time to try out new recipes and prepare delicious dishes or treats. Experiment with spices and ingredients and let your culinary imagination run wild.

Dance or exercise: Dance to your favorite music, practice yoga, do dance choreography, or go for a walk. Exercise can not only stimulate your creativity, but also reduce stress and increase your well-being.

Arts and Crafts: Engage in various forms of arts and crafts such as candle making, jewelry design, mosaic art, or collage. Let your imagination and dexterity work together.

Participating in creative activities during alone time can give you a deep sense of joy, relaxation, and self-actualization. Experiment with different forms of creative expression and find out which ones inspire and fulfill you the most. Don't be too hard on yourself and allow yourself to get lost in the creative process and discover new things.

4.3.4 Nature and movement

Connecting with nature and being physically active can be wonderful ways to invigorate your body and mind during alone time. Here are some suggestions for how you can explore nature and get physical exercise:

Walks in nature: Go to nearby parks, forests or the beach and enjoy a relaxing walk in nature. Breathe in the fresh air, listen to the sounds of nature and consciously notice the beauty of your surroundings.

Hiking: Plan longer hikes in nature to discover new landscapes and challenge your body. Hiking not only provides physical exercise, but also the opportunity to quiet the mind and relieve stress.

Cycling: Take a bike ride around town or explore scenic bike paths in nature. Cycling can be an enjoyable way to exercise and allow you to explore your surroundings.

Outdoor yoga: Find a quiet place outdoors, spread out your yoga mat and practice yoga or meditation. Connecting with nature can calm your mind and deepen your yoga practice.

Water sports: try activities like swimming, kayaking, or stand-up paddling when you're near bodies of water. Water sports offer not only fun and physical activity, but also a connection to the natural environment.

Gardening: Use your alone time to take care of your garden. Plant new flowers, vegetables or herbs, take care of your plants and enjoy working with the soil.

Nature Sketching or Photography: Take a sketchbook or camera and document the beauty of nature. Draw, paint or photograph your impressions and take time to capture the details and features of the natural environment.

Connecting with nature and being physically active can help you relieve stress, increase your sense of well-being, and awaken your senses. Use your alone time to explore nature and get moving. Feel the healing benefits of nature and enjoy the positive effects on your body and mind.

4.3.5 Meditation and mindfulness

Meditation and mindfulness exercises are wonderful tools for finding inner peace and serenity during alone time. They help you become aware of the moment and let go of negative thoughts and worries. Here are some ways you can incorporate meditation and mindfulness into your alone time:

Breath-based meditation: Sit in a quiet place, close your eyes and focus on your breath. Watch the breath flow in and out, and let go of all other thoughts. If your thoughts wander, gently bring your attention back to the breath.

Walking meditation: Walk slowly and deliberately while focusing on each step and movement. Feel the ground beneath your feet, the air on your skin, and the sounds around you. Quiet your thoughts and be fully in the present moment.

Body scan meditation: Lie down comfortably and focus on different parts of your body, from your toes to your head. Consciously feel each part of your body, identify any tension or discomfort, and release it with each exhalation.

Mindful eating: Take time to consciously enjoy your meals. Notice the aromas, textures and tastes of the food. Chew slowly and completely and be fully aware of food intake.

Mindfulness exercises: Perform short mindfulness exercises throughout the day. Pay conscious attention to your sensory perceptions, whether it's the sound of birds, the feel of the wind on your skin, or the taste of a cup of tea.

Guided Meditations: Use guided meditations to help you get into a relaxed and mindful state. There are many meditation apps and online resources that can help you do this.

The practice of meditation and mindfulness can help you live in the moment with awareness, reduce stress, and strengthen your inner peace. Experiment with different techniques and find out which ones suit you best. Incorporate mindfulness into your alone time and consciously take moments of stillness and presence for yourself.

4.3.6 Social interaction

Although the book deals with being alone, it is important to recognize that social interaction is an essential part of a fulfilling life. During your alone time, you should still find ways to socialize and connect with others. Here are some ideas on how to incorporate social interaction into your alone time:

Phone calls or video conferences: Take time to talk on the phone or make video calls with family, friends, or other close people. Share your thoughts, experiences and emotions with them and listen carefully when they do the same. These interactions can create a sense of connection and sharing.

Participate in group activities: Search for interest groups or communities that meet online or offline. These can be reading circles, hobby groups, discussion forums, or sports clubs. Get involved in such activities to meet new people and share common interests.

Volunteer: Get involved in volunteer work or support local non-profit organizations. Not only can you help others, but you can also socialize and make new friends.

Attend cultural events: Go alone to cultural events such as theater performances, concerts, art exhibitions, or readings. While enjoying these events, there is an opportunity to talk with other people and discover common interests.

Online communities: Join online communities, forums, or discussion groups that deal with topics that interest you. Share your opinions, ideas, and experiences with others and use the platform to foster social interactions.

While alone, it is important to still socialize and connect with others. Find ways to stay in touch with others, whether virtually or in person. Social interaction can help you maintain relationships, make new connections, and experience a sense of belonging.

4.3.7 Self-reflection and diary writing

Alone time provides a valuable opportunity for self-reflection and journaling. These practices allow you to explore your thoughts and feelings, gain clarity, and get to know yourself better. Here are some approaches to incorporating self-reflection and journaling into your alone time:

Daily journal writing: Take time regularly to record your thoughts, emotions, and experiences in a journal. Write freely from your mind without worrying about grammar or spelling. Let your thoughts flow and reflect on your experiences, challenges, and progress.

Self-reflection questions: Ask yourself questions that promote your personal development. Ask yourself what is important to you, what your goals are, and what steps you can take to achieve those goals. Reflect on your strengths, weaknesses, and values. Answering such questions can help you gain clarity and find your direction in life.

Meditation and introspection: Use alone time to sit in silence and observe yourself. Pay attention to your thoughts, feelings, and bodily sensations without judging or analyzing them. Simply allow awareness of yourself to arise and observe the flow of your inner experiences.

Reflect on experiences: Use alone time to reflect on and learn from past experiences. Ask yourself what you learned from certain situations, how you moved forward, and how you can act differently in the future. Consciously reflecting on past experiences can help you grow personally and deepen your understanding of yourself.

Create a vision board or collage: Create a vision board or collage to visually represent your goals, dreams and aspirations. Collect images, quotes or symbols that inspire, motivate and remind you of your goals. Place your vision board in a place where you can see it regularly to remind yourself of what you are working for.

The practices of self-reflection and journaling open you to a space of self-knowledge and growth. Use alone time to connect with your thoughts, feelings and goals in this way. By better understanding and reflecting on yourself, you can further your journey of personal development.

4.3.8 Set limits

During alone time, it's important to set boundaries to respect your needs and truly enjoy your alone time. Here are some practical tips on how to set boundaries:

Communicate your needs: Communicate to others that you need time for yourself and that you do not want to be disturbed during this time. Be clear in your communication and explain why this time is important to you.

Create physical boundaries: Establish an area in your home that serves as your personal space for alone time. Make sure this area is respected by others and that you remain undisturbed. Close the door, hang a "do not disturb" sign, or find other ways to maintain your physical privacy.

Set time limits for social media and technology: In our connected world, it's easy to get caught up in endless online activity. Set clear time limits for social media, email and other technology activities to ensure you have enough time for yourself.

Learn to say "no": Be prepared to say "no" when you are offered activities or invitations that may interfere with your alone time. It is important to prioritize your own needs and allow yourself to have time to yourself.

Delegate or ask for assistance: If you have responsibilities or tasks that prevent you from having enough alone time, consider delegating them or asking for assistance. Learn to pass on responsibilities and accept help to allow yourself time for yourself.

Be mindful of your energy: Be mindful of your own energy and boundaries. If you feel overwhelmed or overstimulated, take the time you need to recharge and restore your boundaries.

By setting boundaries, you show others and yourself that your alone time is important and that you respect it. Setting boundaries is an act of self-care and allows you to take full advantage of being alone.

4.3.9 Professional support

Sometimes feelings of loneliness may have deeper causes or be more difficult to cope with. In such cases, it can be helpful to seek professional support. Here are some ways you can get professional help:

Therapy: seek out a qualified therapist or psychologist who specializes in loneliness and personal development. Therapy can help you better understand your feelings, gain new perspectives, and develop coping strategies.

Counseling: find a counseling center or life coach who can help you cope with loneliness. An experienced counselor can help you explore your feelings, improve your relationship skills, and find new ways to make social connections.

Support groups: Inquire about support groups or support groups that address issues such as loneliness, personal growth, or social interaction. Sharing with people who are going through similar experiences can provide valuable support.

Online resources: Use online resources such as forums, websites, or apps that provide information and support related to loneliness and personal development. Here you can benefit from expert advice, share experiences with others, and discover new strategies for coping with loneliness.

Crisis phone or hotlines: If you are in an acute crisis or need to talk to someone urgently, there are phone hotlines and emergency numbers that are available 24/7. Don't be afraid to call on these resources if you need support.

It is important to realize that there is no shame in seeking professional help. Sometimes it's exactly what we need to help us cope with loneliness and personal challenges. Be open to this possibility and don't be afraid to ask for support when you need it.

4.4 The search for community and social support despite being alone

Although being alone can be a valuable time of self-reflection and personal development, it is also important to find community and social support. Here are some ways you can seek community and receive social support despite being alone:

Interest groups and clubs: Find interest groups or clubs that deal with topics that interest you. These can be sports clubs, book clubs, creative groups, or other communities. Join such groups to meet people with similar interests and do activities together.

Volunteer: Get involved in non-profit organizations or volunteer projects. This not only gives you the opportunity to help others, but also to make new contacts and be part of a social community. Look for projects that match your values and interests.

Local events: Find out about local events such as lectures, workshops, concerts or exhibitions in your area. Go there alone and be open to meeting new people. There are often meet-up groups or networking events that focus specifically on getting to know like-minded people.

Online communities: Use online communities, forums or social media to exchange ideas with like-minded people and make new contacts. There are numerous platforms where you can find people who have similar interests or experiences. However, be careful and make sure that the communities are reputable and safe.

Courses and training: Sign up for classes or continuing education in areas that interest you. This could be a language course, a dance class, an art workshop, or something completely different. These classes are often a great way to meet people with similar interests and grow together in something new.

Neighborhood and local community: Get involved in your neighborhood or local community. Attend neighborhood meetings, street fairs, or other events. It is often easier to connect with people in your immediate area and build a supportive social network.

Despite being alone, there are many ways to find community and social support. Be open to meeting new people, get actively involved in your neighborhood, and find ways to connect with others. Community and social connections are important resources that can enrich your well-being and quality of life.

5. The relationship with others: The balance between being alone and being with others

5.1 The importance of relationships and social connectedness

Relationships and social connectedness play a significant role in our lives. They contribute significantly to our well-being, mental health and life satisfaction. Here are some reasons why relationships and social connectedness are so important:

Emotional support: Relationships provide us with emotional support. We can open up to our friends, family members or partners, share our worries and fears, and find comfort in difficult times. Sharing emotional support strengthens our resilience and helps us cope better with stress.

Sharing joy and experiences: In relationships, we can share our joy, successes and milestones. Celebrating successes together gives meaning to our lives and makes us feel connected and happy. By sharing positive experiences, we can multiply our joy.

Support in difficult times: Relationships are a source of comfort and support during difficult times. When we face challenges, be it job stress, health problems or personal crises, supportive relationships can help us cope better with these challenges.

Social identity and belonging: Relationships play an important role in the development of our social identity and our belonging to communities. Through our relationships, we can feel connected to others, feel accepted and understood, and know our own identity is strengthened.

Strengthening mental health: Social connectedness has a positive impact on our mental health. Relationships can alleviate loneliness and isolation, reduce depressive symptoms, and increase overall well-being. Sharing thoughts, feelings and experiences in relationships can have a therapeutic effect.

Meaningful Relationships: Relationships can give us a sense of meaning and purpose in life. By caring for others, providing support, and having a positive impact on the lives of others, we feel needed and have a sense that our lives have deeper meaning.

It is important to cultivate relationships and seek social connectedness as they contribute to our personal growth, well-being and life satisfaction. Invest time and energy in developing and maintaining meaningful relationships to experience the many positive aspects of social connectedness.

5.2 The art of setting healthy boundaries and creating time for yourself

In the midst of our social interactions and relationships, it's important to set healthy boundaries and create time for ourselves. Here are some thoughts and tips on how we can master the art of self-care and time management:

Recognize your needs: Take time to identify and understand your own needs. Ask yourself what kind of time is important to you and how much social interaction you need to feel balanced and comfortable.

Set clear boundaries: Learn to communicate your boundaries and respect them. Kindly but firmly let others know when you need time for yourself or when certain activities or social interactions cross your boundaries. By communicating your boundaries clearly and respectfully, you give others the opportunity to understand and accept your needs.

Time management: Consciously create time for yourself in your everyday life. Schedule regular windows of time when you can be alone and focus on your own needs. This may mean reducing or delegating certain activities to allow time for rest, relaxation or self-care.

Prioritize self-care: Make self-care a priority. Identify activities that energize you, help you unwind, and promote your well-being. These can be things like reading, walking in nature, mediation, sports, or creative activities. Consciously schedule these activities and take them seriously.

Learn to say "no": It is important to learn to say "no" when you feel overwhelmed or when activities cross your boundaries. Allow yourself to detach and free yourself from commitments that don't do you any good or overwhelm you. Remember that it's okay to prioritize your needs and protect yourself.

Create a supportive environment: To set healthy boundaries and create time for yourself, it is helpful to have a supportive environment. Surround yourself with people who respect and support your needs. This may mean intentionally cultivating friendships and relationships that give you space for self-care.

The art of setting healthy boundaries and creating time for yourself requires self-reflection, self-awareness, and a willingness to take care of yourself. By recognizing your needs, setting clear boundaries, and prioritizing time for yourself, you can live a balanced and fulfilling life that incorporates both social connectedness and individual self-care.

5.3 Strengthening relationships through individual development

Relationships are not static, but are constantly evolving. One way to strengthen relationships is to focus on individual development. Here are some approaches to how personal development can help strengthen relationships:

Self-reflection: Through self-reflection, you can develop a deeper understanding of yourself. By recognizing your own strengths, weaknesses, values and needs, you can also communicate more clearly in relationships and empathize better with others. Self-reflection enables you to act more consciously in relationships and to do your part for mutual support and growth.

Personal development: Individual personal development contributes to your own maturity and self-development. By working on your skills, knowledge and emotional growth, you strengthen your resources and bring an enriching perspective to relationships. Through continuous personal development, you expand your potential, which can also make relationships deeper and more fulfilling.

Empathy and understanding: By working on your empathy skills, you are better able to understand other people's perspectives and respond compassionately. This promotes understanding in relationships and creates an atmosphere of trust and openness.

Through empathy, you show that you care about the feelings and needs of others, which improves the quality of interpersonal connections.

Open communication: Individual development can help improve communication skills. By working on your ability to express your thoughts, needs, and desires clearly and respectfully, you promote open and honest communication in relationships. Open communication creates space for mutual growth and solution finding, while misunderstandings and conflicts can be reduced.

Shared goals and interests: Through your individual development, you have the opportunity to explore and pursue your interests, passions, and goals. By sharing your own experiences and accomplishments with others, you can strengthen connection in relationships. Shared interests and goals create space for common activities and allow you to dive deeper into relationships.

Strengthening relationships through individual development requires self-reflection, commitment, and a willingness to continually work on yourself. By working on your personal development, you not only contribute to your own growth, but also to a deeper connection and fulfilling exchange with others.

5.4 Expanding the social network and maintaining friendships

Expanding your social network and maintaining friendships are important aspects of fostering social connectedness and support. Here are some approaches to expand your social network and maintain existing friendships:

Openness to new contacts: Be open to new encounters and enjoy meeting new people. Get involved in activities and interest groups that match your preferences and take advantage of opportunities to make new contacts. Be curious and open-minded about other people and their experiences.

Quality over quantity: It's not just about having a large number of friends, but more importantly about cultivating quality relationships. Focus on building genuine connections and developing friendships based on trust, respect and mutual support.

Active communication: Maintain your friendships through regular and active communication. Take time to talk with your friends, whether in person, by phone, or digitally. Show interest in their lives, their experiences, and their concerns. Also show your own authenticity and share your thoughts and feelings.

Shared activities: Plan shared activities with your friends, whether it's a meal together, an outing, a hobby, or a cultural event. By sharing positive experiences and adventures, you strengthen bonds and create shared memories.

Support and empathy: Show support and empathy toward your friends. Be willing to listen to them, offer help when needed, and acknowledge their successes and challenges. Show understanding of their feelings and needs and be there for them when they need you.

Invest time and energy: Friendships require time and energy. Make a conscious effort to take time to stay connected with and care about your friends. Schedule meetings and activities to nurture and strengthen the relationship. Invest in the friendships that are important to you.

Openness to diversity: Be open to diversity and different types of friendships. Everyone is unique and brings different perspectives and experiences. Open up to people from different backgrounds and walks of life to enrich your social network.

Expanding your social network and cultivating friendships requires your commitment and willingness to invest time and energy. By actively working on your relationships, you can build a supportive social network and experience fulfilling social connectedness.

6. Loneliness in a networked world: digital media and being alone

6.1 The impact of social media and technology on loneliness

In today's connected world, technology plays an increasingly important role in our daily lives. While social media and technology can offer many benefits, there are also potential implications for loneliness. Here are some aspects to consider:

Superficial relationships: Social media allows us to stay in touch with a wide range of people. However, these relationships can often be superficial and based only on likes, comments and virtual interactions. This can make it difficult to build real emotional connections and cultivate deeper relationships.

Fear of Missing Out (FOMO): The constant availability of information on social media can make us feel like we are missing out if we are not constantly online. This can lead to a constant need to stay up to date and not miss an activity or event. This constant comparison and feeling of missing out can lead to feelings of loneliness.

Digital filter bubble: Social media algorithms tend to show us content that matches our preferences and interests. This can result in a limited view and a limited diversity of opinions. This can affect social connectedness, as we may interact less with people who have different views and experiences.

Cyberbullying and negative feedback: A dark side of social media is the possibility of cyberbullying and negative feedback. Experiencing online bullying or negative comments can lead to feelings of exclusion, shame, and loneliness. The anonymity of the Internet can make people less likely to hold back and post negative comments.

Comparison with others: Social media makes it easy to see other people's lives and compare them to our own. This constant comparison can lead to feelings of dissatisfaction, low self-esteem, and loneliness when we feel that our lives don't measure up to others.

It is important to be aware of how social media and technology can affect our feelings of loneliness. This does not mean that social media and technology are inherently negative, but that we should be aware of their impact and make conscious choices about how we use them. Taking digital breaks, having more intentional online interactions, and cultivating real social connections outside of the virtual world can be helpful in counteracting feelings of loneliness.

6.2 The conscious use of digital media to promote being alone

In an increasingly connected world, digital media play an ever greater role in our everyday lives. But instead of letting them overwhelm us, we can learn to use them consciously to enhance and enrich our aloneness. This chapter is dedicated to exploring different ways we can purposefully use digital media to positively shape our aloneness.

Digital media offer numerous opportunities to connect with other people, even when we are physically alone. Social networks and online communities allow us to find like-minded people and share our interests and experiences with them. We can use forums, groups or platforms to engage in discussions, make new friends or even find mentors to support us in our personal development.

But it's not just about connecting with other people. Digital media also offer us the opportunity to get to know ourselves better and to use our alone time to develop ourselves further. We can use online courses and tutorials to learn new skills or deepen our passions. There are a variety of apps and programs that can help us with self-reflection and mindfulness practice. We can keep digital journals, use meditation apps, or attend virtual retreats to embark on our inner journey and strengthen our self-connection.

However, it is important to maintain a balance and not lose ourselves in the digital world. Therefore, we should consciously decide how much time we spend in virtual spaces and which activities really fulfill us. It can be helpful to set clear boundaries and determine times when we are consciously offline to create space for being alone without digital distractions.

Consciously using digital media to promote aloneness requires mindfulness and self-reflection. It's about looking at media as tools to help us enjoy our aloneness, evolve, and connect with others when we want to. By consciously using these technologies, we can get the best of both worlds - digital and real - for our fulfilling aloneness.

This chapter presents concrete strategies and tips on how we can use digital media specifically to enrich our alone time. It's about building a healthy and balanced relationship with digital media and using it as a tool to support our individual needs and goals.

6.3 The dangers of excessive screen time and virtual isolation

Although digital media offers many opportunities to enrich being alone, it is also important to recognize the potential dangers of excessive screen time and virtual isolation. Here are some risks that may be associated with excessive use of digital media:

Isolation and social alienation: Excessive use of digital media can lead to an isolated lifestyle in which real social interactions are neglected. The virtual world cannot provide the same level of human connection and social support as face-to-face encounters. This can lead to increasing social alienation and loneliness.

Health effects: Excessive screen time can lead to a variety of health problems, including sleep disturbance, eye strain, postural damage, and physical inactivity. These health effects can affect well-being and negatively impact being alone.

Comparison and negative self-presentation: Due to the constant presence of social media, we can find ourselves in constant comparison with other people. This can lead to low self-esteem, self-doubt, and the need to present a perfect life. The digital world can provide a distorted representation of reality and self-images, which can lead to negative effects on being alone.

Information overload and distraction: Constantly receiving notifications and having information at your fingertips can lead to brain overload. This can affect the ability to relax and focus on being alone. The constant distraction can make it difficult to enjoy the moment and immerse yourself in your inner world.

It's important to maintain a conscious approach to digital media to minimize negative effects on being alone. Set limits on screen time, create time-outs from the digital world, and invest in real-world social interactions and personal experiences. Conscious use of digital media can be an asset to being alone, but it's critical to find a balance and maintain a connection to the real world.

6.4 The balance between online interaction and personal presence

In an increasingly digital world, it's important to strike a healthy balance between online interaction and in-person presence. Here are some ways you can achieve that balance:

Conscious online scheduling: Set clear boundaries for the time you spend online. Plan intentional times to devote to digital media and times to go offline to enjoy personal interactions and experiences.

Quality online interaction: Make sure your online interactions are meaningful and enriching. Avoid superficial or incriminating content and focus on interactions with people who make positive contributions and inspire you. Cultivate genuine connections by actively engaging in conversations and showing genuine interest in others.

Prioritize face-to-face encounters: Give priority to face-to-face encounters. Use digital communication as a supplement to stay in touch with people who are farther away, but still strive to arrange face-to-face meetings and shared activities. Face-to-face interactions offer a deeper level of connection and allow you to experience nonverbal cues and emotions.

Offline activities: Intentionally make time for activities that connect you offline to the real world. This can mean spending time in nature, reading a book, being artistic, or playing sports. These activities encourage solitude and provide space for personal growth and development.

Mindfulness and self-reflection: Be aware of how you use digital media and how it affects your well-being. Take regular breaks to look inside yourself, reflect on your needs, and focus on your own presence. Mindfulness helps you find the balance between the virtual and real worlds.

By consciously balancing online interaction with in-person presence, you can make being alone a positive experience while cultivating valuable social relationships and personal experiences. It's about using the digital world as a tool to enrich being alone while appreciating real life and personal connection.

7. The Spiritual Dimension of Being Alone: Solitude as a Source of Self-Transcendence

7.1 The connection between being alone and spiritual growth

Being alone can provide a unique opportunity to connect with one's inner self and foster spiritual growth. Here are some aspects that illustrate the connection between being alone and spiritual growth:

Inner silence and mindfulness: Being alone allows us to leave behind the noise and distractions of the outer world and focus on inner silence. In this state of mindfulness, we can dive deep within ourselves and connect more deeply to our spiritual core.

Self-reflection and self-knowledge: Being alone creates space for self-reflection and self-knowledge. By distancing ourselves from outside influences, we can focus on our thoughts, feelings and life experiences. We can consciously confront our values, beliefs, and spiritual needs, thus enhancing our spiritual growth.

Connecting with nature and the universe: Being alone offers us the opportunity to connect with nature and the universe. By spending time outdoors, we can perceive the beauty of the natural world and feel a deeper connection with it. We can also consciously open ourselves to the larger questions of life and develop a sense of connection with the universe.

Practices of silence and meditation: Being alone can create the space for practical practices such as silence and meditation. These practices allow us to quiet our thoughts, still the mind, and open ourselves to higher levels of consciousness. Through regular practice, we can deepen our spiritual practice and develop a deeper understanding of our own spirituality.

Broadening awareness and perspective: Being alone opens up the possibility of looking beyond our own horizons and taking on new perspectives. By distancing ourselves from outside influences, we can rely on our inner wisdom and intuition to gain new knowledge and insight. This expanded awareness can lead to deeper spiritual growth.

Thus, being alone can serve as a valuable tool for spiritual growth. It allows us to focus on our inner world, strengthen our connection to nature and the universe, and deepen with our own spirituality. By using being alone as a time of self-reflection, silence, and mindfulness, we can enhance our spiritual growth and create a deeper connection to ourselves and the greater whole.

7.2 The Search for Meaning and Life Fulfillment in Aloneness

Being alone provides a unique opportunity to address one's own search for meaning and life fulfillment. Here are some aspects that illustrate the connection between being alone and the search for meaning:

Inner reflection and self-knowledge: Being alone allows us to detach from external distractions and focus on our inner thoughts, values and goals. Through this inner reflection we can better understand who we are, what is important to us, and what goals and values fill our lives.

Clarification of one's priorities: Being alone gives us the opportunity to reevaluate our priorities and focus on what's important. By distancing ourselves from outside influences, we can find out what is really important to us and what fulfills us. This allows us to make conscious decisions that are in line with our personal values and goals.

Discovery and development of personal passions: In solitude, we have space and time to explore and develop our interests and passions. By focusing on our own needs and inclinations, we can discover what brings us joy and fulfills us. Being alone can encourage us to try new hobbies, find creative expression, or deepen our skills in a particular area.

Connection to a greater purpose: Being alone allows us to connect to a greater purpose or meaning. By taking time to reflect on our values and how we want to live our lives, we can consciously align ourselves with a mission or purpose that gives us fulfillment and meaning. This may mean committing to social or environmental causes or helping others in individual ways.

The importance of relationships: When we are alone, we also recognize the importance of relationships to our life fulfillment. Although we find ourselves in moments of aloneness, we understand that relationships with others can make a valuable contribution to our well-being and life fulfillment. Being alone can encourage us to build intentional relationships, develop our interpersonal skills, and seek support and connection in our social environment.

The search for meaning and life fulfillment in solitude is an individual journey that requires time, self-reflection, and a willingness to examine one's own values, goals, and needs. Being alone allows us to focus on what truly fulfills us and leads us on the path to a meaningful life.

7.3 The Practice of Meditation and Mindfulness for Deeper Self-Connection

The practice of meditation and mindfulness offers a valuable way to establish a deeper connection with oneself and live a fulfilling life on one's own. Here are some aspects that illustrate the importance of meditation and mindfulness for deeper self-connection:

Inner stillness and mindfulness: Through the practice of meditation we can quiet the mind and achieve a state of inner stillness. In this state, we have the opportunity to consciously focus on the present moment and develop mindfulness. By observing our thoughts and feelings without holding on to them or judging them, we can establish a deeper connection with ourselves.

Self-observation and self-knowledge: The regular practice of meditation and mindfulness enables us to better observe and understand ourselves. By observing our thoughts, feelings, and physical sensations, we can develop a deeper understanding of our inner processes. This self-knowledge enables us to break free from limiting patterns and beliefs and to develop our full potential.

Acceptance and compassion: Through the practice of mindfulness, we learn to approach ourselves with acceptance and compassion. Instead of judging or criticizing ourselves, we can learn to accept ourselves as we are, with all our strengths and weaknesses. This loving attitude toward ourselves promotes a deeper self-connection and a sense of wholeness.

Connection with the body: Through mindful awareness of the body, we can establish a deeper connection with ourselves. By consciously using our senses and focusing on the physical sensations in the present moment, we can feel connected to our body and experience a sense of oneness. This body connection allows us to be more aware of our needs and limitations and to take care of our physical well-being.

Expanding Consciousness: Through the practice of meditation and mindfulness, we can expand our consciousness and establish a deeper connection to our true self. By releasing ourselves from limiting identifications with the ego and directing our consciousness into a state of presence and spaciousness, we can unfold our inner potential and experience a deeper self-connection.

The practice of meditation and mindfulness thus provides us with tools to recognize ourselves on a deeper level and establish a deeper connection with ourselves. Through regular practice, we can experience a sense of wholeness, clarity, and inner peace that helps us appreciate being alone as a valuable and fulfilling experience.

7.4 The integration of spirituality into the everyday life of being alone

Integrating spirituality into everyday life of being alone can help find deeper meaning and fulfillment. Here are some approaches to integrating spirituality into the daily routine of being alone:

Rituals and Meditation: Establishing rituals and regular meditation practices can provide a connection to a higher power or transcendent meaning. By creating a sacred space and incorporating rituals such as lighting candles, reciting prayers or affirmations, or performing meditative practices, we can create a spiritual atmosphere and deepen our connection to the divine.

Connecting with Nature: Nature offers a rich source of spiritual experience. By spending time in nature, we can connect with the beauty and wonder of the universe. By walking in the forest, watching the sunset, or gazing at the stars, we can establish a deeper connection to nature and the divine.

Self-reflection and introspection: Being alone provides a valuable opportunity for self-reflection and introspection. By consciously taking time to listen within ourselves, we can connect with our inner wisdom and higher self. This can be done through journal writing, meditation, silent contemplation, or other spiritual practices that help us explore our inner knowing and spiritual guidance.

Practicing compassion and love: Spirituality often involves the aspect of compassion and love for oneself and others. Through the conscious practice of compassion and loving kindness, we can open our hearts and experience a deeper connection with all beings. This can be done by sending loving thoughts or prayers, performing good deeds, or engaging in volunteer work.

Study of spiritual texts or philosophies: Reading and studying spiritual texts or philosophies can inspire us and expand spiritual knowledge. By immersing ourselves in the wisdom and teachings of mystics, philosophers, or spiritual teachers, we can gain new insights and deepen our spiritual journey.

Integrating spirituality into the daily routine of being alone allows us to find a deeper connection to our own spirituality and to find meaning in being alone. It can help us strengthen our inner guidance, connect with a higher power, and experience a deep fulfillment and satisfaction that transcends external circumstances.

8. The art of reconnecting: ways out of loneliness

8.1 Strategies for overcoming chronic loneliness

Chronic loneliness can be a challenging experience, but there are several strategies that can help overcome it. Here are some approaches that can help you manage chronic loneliness:

8.1.1 Self-reflection

Self-reflection is an important step in overcoming chronic loneliness. Here are some aspects of self-reflection that can help:

Honestly take stock: take time to honestly reflect and identify your own feelings of loneliness. Ask yourself what exactly you are feeling and what impact loneliness is having on your life.

Identify causes: Try to figure out what factors might be contributing to your chronic loneliness. It could be circumstances such as moving, losing friends or loved ones, or a change in your living situation. Identify these causes so you can work on them.

Understanding needs: Explore your own needs and desires. Ask yourself what is important to you in social relationships and what you hope to get out of them. Identify other aspects of your life that can bring you joy and fulfillment, independent of social interaction.

Personal development: Use your alone time to develop yourself and discover your personal strengths and interests. Set goals and pursue them, whether professional, creative, or in other areas. Through personal growth, you can strengthen your self-esteem and increase your attractiveness to others.

Challenge negative thinking patterns: Review your thinking patterns about loneliness. Often people tend to have negative thoughts about themselves when they feel lonely. Identify these negative thought patterns and try to replace them with positive and constructive thoughts.

Self-love and self-care: Strengthen your relationship with yourself by practicing self-love and self-care. Accept yourself as you are and treat yourself with kindness and compassion. Do things that bring you joy and give you a sense of fulfillment.

Self-reflection opens up a way for you to get to know yourself better and to address your own needs. By consciously working on your personal development and questioning your thought patterns, you can better understand your loneliness and work specifically to overcome it.

8.1.2 Social activities

Social activities play an important role in overcoming chronic loneliness. Here are some approaches to social activities that can help you:

Community Events: Find out about local events that match your interests. For example, attend concerts, art exhibits, sporting events, or readings. These events are a great way to meet people with similar interests and make new contacts.

Courses and workshops: Sign up for classes or workshops that pique your curiosity. Whether it's a dance class, a cooking class, a language course, or a craft group, such activities give you the opportunity to connect with other participants and share common experiences.

Volunteer: Get involved with nonprofit organizations or projects that are close to your heart. Volunteering not only allows you to help others, but also to meet like-minded people and build social bonds.

Sports and Fitness Groups: Join a sports group, gym, or running club. A shared interest in physical activity creates a natural basis for social interaction and offers the opportunity to make new friends.

Meetup Groups: Explore online platforms like Meetup to find groups that match your interests and hobbies. There are a variety of groups that meet regularly to do activities together. Whether it's a hiking group, a book club, or a discussion group on a particular topic, such groups give you the opportunity to meet like-minded people and make new social connections.

Social media: Use social media to share your interests and socialize with others. There are several online communities and groups where you can find people who have similar interests. Be active and engage in discussions and activities to make new connections.

It is important to note that it takes some time and openness to make new social connections. Be patient and don't give up. Engage in social activities regularly to increase your chances of meeting new people and overcoming your loneliness.

8.1.3 Volunteering

Volunteering can be an enriching experience and help you overcome chronic loneliness. Here are some opportunities and benefits of volunteering:

Charitable Organizations: Find out about local charities that match your interests and values. You can get involved with animal shelters, soup kitchens, hospitals, nursing homes, or environmental organizations. Working with other volunteers and helping those in need creates a meaningful connection and makes you feel part of a community.

Community Projects: Get involved in community projects like cleaning parks, organizing events, or supporting educational initiatives. Together with other volunteers, you can make positive changes in your neighborhood while making new contacts.

Become a mentor or tutor: Share your knowledge and skills by becoming a mentor or tutor. You can help high school students, college students, or individuals with special needs. By sharing your experiences and helping others, you can not only overcome loneliness, but also connect with people in meaningful ways.

Organize community events: Organize community events or activities in collaboration with other volunteers. For example, you can organize a street fair, an art show, or a charity event. This allows you to strengthen your social skills, meet new people, and create something positive together.

International volunteering: If you have a sense of adventure, you can also participate in international volunteering programs. There are organizations that offer volunteering abroad, be it in education, healthcare or environmental protection. This allows you to learn about new cultures, broaden your perspective, and connect with people from all over the world.

Volunteering gives you the opportunity to use your skills and help others while building social bonds. You can become part of a community working toward similar goals while experiencing a sense of belonging and significance. By investing your time and energy in volunteering, you can overcome loneliness and feel like you are making a positive contribution to society.

8.1.4 Online communities

In the digital era, online communities offer a way to overcome loneliness and meet like-minded people. Here are some benefits and ways online communities can help you:

Forums and discussion groups: There are a variety of forums and discussion groups on just about any topic that interests you. Join an online community where people have similar interests and discuss relevant topics. You can ask questions, share opinions, and get valuable information. By actively participating, you can socialize and interact with others in a supportive environment.

Social media: Platforms like Facebook, Twitter, Instagram, and LinkedIn provide opportunities to connect with people who have similar interests, hobbies, or career goals. Search for groups, pages, or events that match your interests and participate in discussions or organize meetings with other members. Social networks allow you to build social interactions online and continue your connections offline.

Online courses and webinars: Take online courses or webinars to learn new skills or deepen your knowledge in a specific area. In these virtual learning environments, you have the opportunity to interact with other participants, ask questions, and share common interests. This creates a community of learners who support and learn from each other.

Gaming community: If you like playing video games, you can join a gaming community. There are many online platforms where you can interact with other gamers, play together, and share strategies and experiences. Gaming communities offer the opportunity to have fun, overcome challenges together, and make friends even if you're physically away from each other.

Dating platforms: If you are looking for romantic relationships, online dating platforms can give you the opportunity to meet potential partners. These platforms offer a variety of tools to find people with similar interests and values and make initial contacts. It's important to proceed with caution and protect your personal information, but for many people, online dating platforms have led to meaningful relationships.

However, it is important to note that online communities cannot replace face-to-face contact. Try to find a balance between online interactions and face-to-face meetings to build a deeper connection. Use online communities as a complement to your social life and as a way to meet new people and find support, even if physical distance is a challenge.

8.1.5 Professional support

If chronic loneliness persists and affects your quality of life, seeking professional support can be helpful. Here are some ways professional help can help you overcome loneliness:

Therapy or counseling: A qualified therapist or counselor can help identify and understand the deeper causes of your loneliness. Through conversations and targeted interventions, you can overcome your personal challenges and fears and develop new coping strategies. Therapy can help you strengthen your self-awareness, build self-esteem, and develop healthy relationships.

Support Groups: Support groups provide a platform where people with similar experiences and challenges can come together to support each other. You can seek out specific support groups that address issues such as social isolation, loss, or other situations that may contribute to loneliness. Support groups provide a safe space to share ideas, receive support, and make new connections.

Social work or community programs: Social work or community programs can give you access to resources and support in your local community. Social workers and community organizations can help find social activities, volunteer opportunities, or other ways to strengthen your social connection and make new contacts.

Online resources: there are a variety of online resources designed specifically for people dealing with loneliness and social isolation.

You can search for online forums, chat rooms, or professional counseling services that specialize in loneliness. These online resources offer a convenient way to get support and advice from qualified professionals.

It's important to seek professional help if you feel your loneliness is chronic and affecting your quality of life. An experienced professional can help identify the causes of loneliness, develop coping strategies, and find new ways to make social connections. Remember that seeking help is brave and powerful, and you don't have to go through this process alone.

8.1.6 Self-care

Self-care is an essential part of overcoming chronic loneliness. By treating yourself with loving attention and care, you can strengthen your emotional health and well-being. Here are some self-care strategies that can help you manage loneliness:

Prioritize your needs: Consciously take time for yourself and make sure to meet your own needs. This can mean taking regular breaks, getting enough rest, eating healthy meals, and engaging in regular physical activity. By meeting your basic needs, you strengthen inner stability and improve your well-being.

Self-care routine: develop a regular self-care routine that includes activities that bring you pleasure and help you take good care of yourself. This might include relaxation exercises, meditation, taking a warm bath, reading a book, or listening to soothing music. Find out what activities help you relax and recharge, and make them a regular habit.

Set boundaries: Learn to recognize your own boundaries and communicate them clearly. Say "no" when you feel overwhelmed or your time and energy are already stretched. Respect your own needs and set clear boundaries to protect your resources.

Self-acceptance and self-compassion: Practice self-acceptance and self-compassion by accepting yourself as you are and treating yourself with kindness and understanding. Allow yourself to make mistakes and learn from them, and be patient with yourself during the process of overcoming loneliness.

Positive self-talk: pay attention to your inner dialogues and replace negative self-talk with positive and supportive thoughts. Speak encouragement to yourself and remind yourself that you are valuable and lovable, regardless of your current social situation.

Self-development: Use your alone time to work on your personal development. Set goals, learn new skills, discover passions, and invest in your personal development. By developing yourself, you will strengthen self-confidence and open up new opportunities for social connections.

By treating yourself with love and care, you lay the foundation for positive change. Self-care is a continuous process that helps you overcome your loneliness and improve your well-being.

8.1.7 Patience and acceptance

In overcoming chronic loneliness, it is important to be patient with yourself and accept yourself. Here are some recommendations on how to incorporate patience and acceptance into your process:

Trust the process: Overcoming chronic loneliness takes time and commitment. Trust that you will make progress step by step, even if there are sometimes setbacks. Be patient with yourself and allow yourself to move forward slowly but steadily.

Accept your feelings: Loneliness can bring up unpleasant emotions, such as sadness, frustration, or fear. Accept these feelings as part of your range of experience and allow yourself to feel them without judging yourself for them. Avoid suppressing or ignoring your feelings, but embrace them and consider them valuable information about your needs.

Be kind to yourself: Talk to yourself in a loving and supportive way. Remind yourself that it is normal to feel lonely sometimes and that you are not alone in these feelings. Be patient with yourself and allow yourself to make mistakes and learn from them.

Seek support: It can be helpful to seek support from other people, whether friends, family members, or professional helpers. Share your experiences, feelings, and challenges with trusted people and let them support and encourage you. Together, you can find ways to cope with your loneliness and build new social connections.

Practice mindfulness: Stay in the present moment and consciously notice your thoughts, feelings and body sensations without judging or condemning them. Mindfulness can help you get to know yourself better, deal with emotions, and take on new perspectives.

Celebrate small progress: Be proud of yourself for every small step forward you make. Celebrate your successes, no matter how small, and encourage yourself to continue actively working on your solitude.

Patience and acceptance are critical factors on your path to overcoming loneliness. Give yourself time, space and love as you grow and make new social connections.

8.2 Building new social contacts and relationships

To build new social contacts and relationships, it's important that you take action and step out of your comfort zone. Here are some tips that can help you do that:

Be open to new encounters: Approach other people with a positive attitude and be open to making new acquaintances. Be curious and interested in the people around you.

Get involved in community activities: Look for activities or groups that match your interests. These can be sports clubs, creative workshops, volunteer projects or other hobbies. There you have the opportunity to meet people with similar interests and share common experiences.

Use social media and online platforms: The Internet offers a variety of ways to meet new people. Use social media platforms to connect with like-minded people or join online communities that match your interests. However, be mindful and choose reputable and trustworthy platforms.

Visit local events and activities: Find out about events in your area, such as concerts, art exhibits, lectures, or markets. Actively attend such events to meet new people and possibly discover common interests.

Get involved in social projects: Get involved in social projects or volunteer work. Not only will you have the opportunity to help others, but you will also meet people who share similar values and are committed to the same causes.

Expand your circle of acquaintances through existing contacts: Use your existing relationships to make new contacts. Ask friends, family members or colleagues if they can introduce you to their circle of friends or if they know of events or meetings where you can meet new people.

Be patient and give yourself time: Building new relationships takes time and patience. Don't be discouraged if things don't work out right away. Give yourself space for the process and be open to new experiences.

By following these tips and actively seeking out new social contacts, you can increase the chance of meeting people who fit your life and build enriching relationships. Trust yourself and be open to the many opportunities life has to offer.

8.3 Active participation in community activities and groups

To expand your social network and meet new people, it's helpful to be actively involved in community activities and groups. Here are some tips that can help you do that:

Find activities that match your interests: Identify areas that interest you and where you enjoy spending time. This could be sports clubs, art groups, book clubs, non-profit organizations, or other communities of interest. Look for groups and activities that reflect your passions and hobbies.

Find out about local events and meetings: Be on the lookout for local events, meetings or gatherings in your area. These can be regulars' tables, networking events, lectures or cultural events. Use online platforms, social media or local advertisements to stay informed about such events.

Get involved in volunteer work: look for opportunities to volunteer. There are many organizations and projects that need your help and support. By volunteering, you can not only do good, but also meet like-minded people who share similar values and interests.

Join groups and clubs: Investigate local groups and clubs that match your interests. There are often sports clubs, hobby groups, reading circles, music ensembles, or other groups you can join.

Participating in regular meetings and activities will allow you to socialize and build new friendships.

Be active and open-minded: Actively approach people and be open to new encounters. Get to know other participants, ask questions, show interest and share your own thoughts and experiences. Participate in discussions, group projects or joint activities to build a deeper connection.

Stay engaged on an ongoing basis: Building relationships takes time and continuity. Try to attend activities and meetings regularly to build a stable presence. The more often you attend, the better you will get to know the other participants and be able to build relationships.

Be patient and open to new experiences: Forming new relationships takes time and patience. Don't be discouraged if close friendships don't form right away. Give yourself and the other participants time to get to know each other and build trust.

By actively participating in community activities and groups, you open up opportunities to meet new people, share common interests, and build supportive relationships. Be willing to get involved and have new experiences, because every encounter can lead to valuable connections.

8.4 Professional support in coping with feelings of loneliness

In the digital world, online communities offer a great way to make social connections and connect with like-minded people. Here are some aspects you can consider when participating in online communities:

Find appropriate online communities: Identify your interests and hobbies and search for appropriate online communities. There are countless platforms, forums, and groups that focus on specific topics. Look for those that best match your interests and needs.

Be active: When you join an online community, be active and participate in discussions, share your knowledge and experiences. Ask questions, contribute new ideas, and support other members. The more you get involved, the better you can build relationships and connect with others.

Respect the community guidelines: Every online community has its own rules and guidelines. Respect them and adhere to the community's standards of conduct. Be friendly, respectful, and avoid offensive or disrespectful comments. A positive and supportive atmosphere contributes to a better community.

Maintain your online relationships: Build relationships with other members by actively interacting with them. Use private messaging, video chats, or other means of communication to interact more personally. Be open to building deeper connections and show interest in the people behind the screens.

Take advantage of offline meetings: When the opportunity arises, meet with other community members offline. Organize joint meetings, meet-ups or events to connect in person. This can be a great opportunity to deepen relationships and develop real friendships.

Be aware of your online safety: Stay alert when using online communities and be aware of your online safety. Don't share personal information with strangers and be careful when clicking on links or downloading files. Trust your gut and report suspicious behavior to community administrators.

Online communities offer a flexible and accessible way to build social connections and be part of a community. Use this resource to meet like-minded people, share ideas, and form supportive relationships. Be active, respectful, and open to new experiences in the online world.

9. Loneliness at different stages of life: Challenges and opportunities

9.1 Loneliness in adolescence and adolescence

The phase of adolescence and youth is a time of great change and challenge. Feelings of loneliness can be particularly strong during this phase of life. Here are some specific aspects of loneliness in adolescence and youth:

Search for identity: Adolescents and young adults are in a phase of identity development in which they are searching for their place in the world. They are trying to figure out who they are, what they like, and where they want to go in life. In this process, loneliness can occur when they feel they are different from others or have difficulty feeling they belong in their environment.

Social comparisons: Social comparisons are particularly present during adolescence. Adolescents often compare themselves to their peers in terms of appearance, popularity, social skills, or achievements. If they feel they don't live up to expectations or don't have enough friends, loneliness can increase.

Peer groups and social pressure: Belonging to a peer group is of great importance to many young people. If they have difficulty making friends or being accepted, this can lead to feelings of loneliness. At the same time, social pressure to fit in or conform to certain norms can also be loneliness-promoting.

Technology and virtual connections: In today's digital era, technology and social media play a major role in the lives of adolescents and young adults. Although they potentially provide opportunities for social networking, they can also lead to feelings of isolation when used as a substitute for face-to-face encounters or lead to excessive comparison and FOMO (Fear of Missing Out).

School and educational institutions: School and educational institutions can be a place where adolescents spend a lot of time and form social relationships. If they have difficulty fitting into their school environment, are bullied, or feel isolated, this can lead to increased feelings of loneliness.

It is important that adolescents and young adults receive support to cope with loneliness during this stage of development. Open communication, building social skills, fostering healthy social relationships, and encouraging self-acceptance can help reduce feelings of loneliness and create a positive social environment. Parents, educators, and youth professionals play an important role in supporting youth in their social and emotional development and helping them find a healthy balance between autonomy and social connectedness.

9.2 Loneliness in adulthood: career, relationships and changes

Adulthood is a phase of life that is associated with various challenges. Feelings of loneliness can occur during this phase of life and can affect different areas of adult life. Here are some specific aspects of loneliness in adulthood:

Career and professional challenges: In adulthood, many people focus on their professional development and career goals. Often this is accompanied by an increased time commitment and stress. If the personal or professional environment does not provide sufficient social support, or if one feels professionally isolated or overwhelmed, loneliness can occur.

Relationships and partnerships: Adulthood is also the time when many people seek romantic relationships and long-term partnerships. Loneliness can occur when people have difficulty finding a suitable partner, maintaining a relationship, or when a relationship ends. In addition, friendships and social networks can change over time, which can lead to feelings of loneliness.

Changes in the social environment: Adulthood is a time of change, when people often have to change their place of residence, lose sight of old friends or establish new social networks. When one is in a new environment or in a phase of life in which the social environment changes, loneliness can set in.

Family obligations and responsibilities: For many adults, adulthood also brings family obligations and responsibilities, whether as parents, caregivers, or supporters of their own family. In the midst of these obligations, it can be difficult to find time for social interactions and building new relationships, which can lead to feelings of loneliness.

It is important to be proactive in dealing with loneliness in adulthood and to develop strategies to strengthen social connections. Engaging in new social activities, maintaining existing relationships, making connections at work, or becoming involved in community service organizations can help reduce feelings of loneliness. In addition, intentionally cultivating self-care and seeking professional support can help with chronic loneliness. By taking these steps, adults can lead fulfilling and socially connected lives.

9.3 Loneliness in old age: challenges and the importance of social ties

As we age, loneliness can become a common challenge. Several factors can contribute to older people feeling lonely. Here are some aspects of loneliness in old age:

Loss of loved ones and friends: As people age, many experience the loss of spouses, siblings, friends, or other loved ones. The loss of social relationships can lead to feelings of loneliness, especially as the social network gradually diminishes.

Mobility limitations: Mobility limitations can occur with age, whether due to physical ailments or age-related limitations. Difficulties in leaving the house or participating in social activities can lead to isolation and loneliness.

Changes in the social environment: Old age is often accompanied by changes in the social environment. Friends may move away or pass away, children may have families of their own and have less time for the older adult. These changes can lead to feelings of isolation.

Health challenges: As people age, their risk for health problems usually increases. Chronic illnesses or physical limitations can affect the ability to participate in social activities and build new relationships.

Social ties and relationships play a crucial role in coping with loneliness in old age. It is important to maintain social contacts and make new ones. This can be done by participating in community activities, senior groups, volunteering, or visiting social centers for older people. Technology and digital media can also provide opportunities to stay in touch with others.

In addition to actively forming social bonds, it is important to maintain one's health, promote physical activity, and develop a positive attitude toward the aging process. Furthermore, the support of professionals, such as social workers or therapists, can be helpful in addressing feelings of loneliness in old age and building a supportive community. Through these interventions, aging can be experienced as a time of fulfillment, social engagement, and positive connections.

9.4 The individual shaping of being alone in different stages of life

Being alone can bring different meanings and challenges at different stages of life. Here are some aspects of individualizing being alone at different stages of life:

Adolescence: Being alone in adolescence can be a time of self-discovery and personal development. Young people have the opportunity to discover their own interests, shape their personalities, and strengthen their individual identities. Being alone can provide space for self-reflection, creativity and personal growth.

Adulthood: In adulthood, professional obligations, partnerships and family responsibilities often take center stage. Nevertheless, it is important to also create time for oneself and enjoy being alone. Alone time can serve to explore one's own needs and desires, pursue personal goals and contribute to self-development.

Parenting: As a parent, being alone can be a rare resource. However, it's important to take time for yourself to recharge your batteries and achieve a work-life balance. Being alone can help relieve stress, maintain one's identity alongside being a parent, and pursue personal interests and passions.

Midlife: Midlife can be a time of change, such as the empty nest, career upheavals, or the transition to retirement. Being alone can be an opportunity to discover new interests, reinvent yourself, and enjoy the freedom to make your own choices. It can also provide space for developing new social contacts and relationships.

Senior years: In senior years, being alone can take on a special meaning. While physical challenges may arise, there is also the opportunity to use being alone as a time for inner peace, spiritual growth and self-reflection. Striving for a balanced combination of being alone and social interaction is important to maintain quality of life and find social support.

At every stage of life, it is important to consciously shape being alone and see it as an opportunity for self-discovery, personal development and fulfillment. Every person has different needs and preferences, so it is crucial to adapt the individual design of being alone to one's own desires and life circumstances.

10.   The Art of Being Alone: A Lifelong Journey

10.1 The continuity of self-discovery and personal development

The journey of self-discovery and personal development does not end with a particular stage of life or experience. Rather, it is a continuous process that can last a lifetime. Here are some important aspects of the continuity of self-discovery and personal development:

Self-reflection: The regular practice of self-reflection allows us to get to know ourselves better, to examine our values and goals, and to enhance our personal growth. It is important to find time for silence and introspection to explore our thoughts, feelings and actions.

Openness to change: A willingness to embrace new experiences, ideas and perspectives is critical to our personal development. By being open to change, we can explore new possibilities, expand our comfort zone and develop ourselves further.

Learning and Continuing Education: The pursuit of continuous learning and education allows us to develop new skills, expand our knowledge, and maintain our mental stimulation. Through books, courses, workshops or other learning opportunities, we can challenge ourselves and discover new horizons.

Flexibility and adaptability: Life is full of changes and challenges. By remaining flexible and adaptable, we can adapt to circumstances, learn from setbacks and strengthen our capacity for resilience. Accepting the unknown and finding solutions to problems are important aspects of personal development.

Self-care: Taking care of our physical, mental and emotional well-being is crucial to our personal development. By taking care of ourselves and treating ourselves with compassion, we can harness our energy and resources for growth and development.

Relationships and support: Our relationships with others play an important role in our personal development. Healthy, supportive relationships provide us with the opportunity to inspire, support and grow with each other. The environment in which we find ourselves can have a major impact on our self-development.

The continuum of self-discovery and personal development requires commitment, patience and the courage to open ourselves to new experiences. It is an ongoing process of growing, learning and understanding that enables us to realize our full potential and live a fulfilling life. By continuously engaging with ourselves and working on our personal development, we can come to a deeper understanding of ourselves and lead an authentic and meaningful existence.

10.2 The integration of aloneness into a fulfilling and balanced life

Being alone can make a valuable contribution to a fulfilling and balanced life if it is integrated consciously and positively. Here are some strategies and approaches to integrate being alone into everyday life:

10.2.1 Self-reflection and self-care

This chapter is about how you can create a healthy and fulfilling life living alone through self-reflection and self-care. Here are some steps you can take:

Take time for yourself: Make it a priority to regularly spend time alone to get to know yourself and identify your needs. Consciously create space for silence and stillness where you can relax and look inward.

Practice self-reflection: examine your thoughts, feelings and experiences. Ask yourself questions like: Who am I really? What are my strengths and weaknesses? What values and goals are important to me? Reflect on your life, your decisions and your relationships. This self-reflection helps you to understand yourself better and to develop yourself further.

Take care of your physical health: Ensure a balanced diet, sufficient sleep and regular physical activity. Ensure sufficient relaxation and stress reduction, be it through meditation, yoga or other relaxation techniques. Your physical well-being has a direct impact on your emotional and mental well-being.

Develop a self-care routine: consciously create routines and rituals that help you take care of yourself. These can be small habits like reading a book, listening to music, writing in a journal, or enjoying a warm bath. Find out what activities and practices give you energy and joy and incorporate them regularly into your daily routine.

Be mindful of yourself: Practice mindfulness by consciously noticing the present moment without judging it. Be loving and compassionate with yourself and accept yourself as you are. Pay attention to your needs and make sure you meet them.

Cultivate positive thoughts and affirmations: Recognize negative thought patterns and work to replace them with positive and supportive thoughts. Use positive affirmations to boost your self-esteem and build a positive self-image.

Set clear boundaries: Learn to recognize and respect your own boundaries. Say no to activities or commitments that are not good for you or drain your energy. Set clear limits on your time, energy and resources.

By practicing self-reflection and self-care, you lay the foundation for a fulfilling and balanced life living alone. Take time for yourself on a regular basis to reflect, care for yourself, and meet your needs. You deserve to be in harmony and in tune with yourself.

10.2.2 Activities and hobbies

Incorporating activities and hobbies into your life can help you enrich being alone and live a full and balanced life. Here are some ideas on how to manage your alone time with activities and hobbies:

Take time for yourself: Make it a priority to regularly spend time alone to get to know yourself and identify your needs. Consciously create space for silence and stillness where you can relax and look inward.

Practice self-reflection: examine your thoughts, feelings and experiences. Ask yourself questions like: Who am I really? What are my strengths and weaknesses? What values and goals are important to me? Reflect on your life, your decisions and your relationships. This self-reflection helps you to understand yourself better and to develop yourself further.

Take care of your physical health: Ensure a balanced diet, sufficient sleep and regular physical activity. Ensure sufficient relaxation and stress reduction, be it through meditation, yoga or other relaxation techniques. Your physical well-being has a direct impact on your emotional and mental well-being.

Develop a self-care routine: consciously create routines and rituals that help you take care of yourself. These can be small habits like reading a book, listening to music, writing in a journal, or enjoying a warm bath. Find out what activities and practices give you energy and joy and incorporate them regularly into your daily routine.

Be mindful of yourself: Practice mindfulness by consciously noticing the present moment without judging it. Be loving and compassionate with yourself and accept yourself as you are. Pay attention to your needs and make sure you meet them.

Cultivate positive thoughts and affirmations: Recognize negative thought patterns and work to replace them with positive and supportive thoughts. Use positive affirmations to boost your self-esteem and build a positive self-image.

Set clear boundaries: Learn to recognize and respect your own boundaries. Say no to activities or commitments that are not good for you or drain your energy. Set clear limits on your time, energy and resources.

By practicing self-reflection and self-care, you lay the foundation for a fulfilling and balanced life living alone. Take time for yourself on a regular basis to reflect, care for yourself, and meet your needs. You deserve to be in harmony and in tune with yourself.

10.2.3 Nature and silence

Connecting with nature and seeking stillness can help integrate being alone into a fulfilling and balanced life. Here are some ways you can incorporate nature and silence into your alone time:

Walks in nature: Take the opportunity to take regular walks in nature. Go to parks, forests or the beach and enjoy the fresh air, green surroundings and soothing sounds of nature. Consciously take time to observe and connect with the beauty of nature.

Gardening: If you have a garden, take the opportunity to spend time outdoors taking care of plants and flowers. Working with soil, watching plants grow, and creating a beautiful garden can give you a sense of fulfillment and harmony.

Meditation in nature: Find quiet places in nature where you can relax and meditate. Sit on a bench, lie down on a blanket, or find a quiet spot under a tree. Close your eyes, breathe deeply in and out, and let the sounds of nature wash over you. This can help you quiet the mind and feel a deeper connection to nature.

Digital timeout in nature: Consciously plan time without digital devices and spend this time in nature. Turn off your cell phone, leave your laptop at home and allow yourself to be in the here and now. Use this time to consciously perceive the beauty of nature, watch birds, feel the wind and catch the scent of flowers.

Enjoy silence: consciously search for places where you can experience silence. These can be quiet places in nature, quiet libraries or secluded parks. Sit in such a place, close your eyes and enjoy the silence around you. Let your thoughts settle and allow yourself to enjoy the moment in its pure stillness.

Nature and silence offer us a space of peace, relaxation and inspiration. By consciously taking time to invite these elements into our lives, we can strengthen our inner connection and come to a sense of serenity and balance. Make time for nature and stillness on a regular basis to recharge your batteries and connect with the beauty and power of the natural world.

10.2.4 Social interaction as needed

Integrating aloneness into a fulfilling and balanced life does not mean completely shutting yourself off from social interaction. Instead, it's about shaping and consciously choosing social interaction as needed. Here are some aspects you can consider in doing so:

Quality over quantity: Focus on having quality social interactions rather than focusing on the number of social contacts. Meet people with whom you feel a deep connection and who support and inspire you. It's not necessary to have a large number of friends as long as you have people in your life who understand and enrich you.

Customize your activities: Choose social activities that meet your needs. If you like interacting in smaller groups, look for intimate gatherings or organize small group activities together. If you prefer to be alone but still want social interaction, you can sign up for group activities where you can meet other people without feeling overwhelmed.

Open communication: Share your social interaction needs and preferences openly with others. Talk about how you prefer to spend your time and what kind of social interaction is good for you. By communicating openly about your needs, you can ensure that your social contacts respect your aloneness and support you.

Flexibility: Be flexible in your social interaction and adapt to different situations. There are times when you want more social interaction and times when you need more time for yourself. Listen to your inner balance and respond accordingly.

Set boundaries: Set clear boundaries to meet your needs for social interaction. Sometimes it's important to say no and set aside time for yourself, even when others invite you to social activities. Learn to communicate your boundaries and make sure you spend enough time alone to maintain your inner balance.

Social interaction on demand means that you consciously decide how much time and energy you want to invest in social activities. It's about recognizing your own needs and acting on them without being pressured by social expectations. Find the right balance between social interaction and being alone to live a fulfilling and balanced life.

10.2.5 Digital detoxification

In an increasingly digitalized world where constant connectivity and screen time are ubiquitous, it's important to also schedule time for a digital detox. This means consciously stepping away from digital devices and online activities to make space for solitude and personal growth. Here are some suggestions for how you can incorporate a digital detox into your life:

Conscious use: Become aware of how much time you spend with digital devices every day. Take stock of your digital habits and identify potential overuse. Set clear limits on your use of social media, online entertainment and other digital platforms.

Screen-free times: Schedule intentional screen-free times to focus on yourself and reduce digital distractions. Use this time to connect with your thoughts, engage in creative activities, or relax in nature.

Digital timeouts: Regularly take extended periods of time off from digital technology. This can be a whole day or even a weekend. Avoid using phones, computers, and other devices, and instead focus on offline activities that you enjoy.

Digital Detox Routines: Integrate regular digital detox routines into your daily routine. These can include daily meditations, mindfulness exercises, or yoga sessions where you consciously shift the focus from digital media to yourself.

Alternative activities: Find alternative activities that take your mind off digital technology and focus your attention elsewhere. This could be sports activities, creative hobbies, reading, talking with friends, or exploring nature. Experiment with different activities and discover what you enjoy.

Mindful digital use: When using digital media, be mindful and selective in your choices. Ask yourself which content is truly valuable and enriching to you and which you might reduce or eliminate. Avoid being caught in endless scrolling loops and instead focus on inspiring and informative content.

A digital detox can help you become more aware and healthy in your relationship with digital media. By allowing yourself alone time without digital distractions, you can deepen your connection to yourself, enhance your creativity, and live a balanced life.

10.2.6 Mindfulness and presence

Another important dimension of integrating aloneness into a fulfilling and balanced life is the practice of mindfulness and presence. By consciously focusing on the present moment and sharpening your senses, you can become more intensely aware of your experiences and connect more deeply with yourself and your surroundings. Here are some ways you can integrate mindfulness and presence into your alone time:

Breathing exercises: Sit in a quiet environment and focus on your breath. Consciously observe the inhalation and exhalation process without controlling it. This will help you stay in the present moment and calm your mind.

Physical awareness: Take time to be aware of your body. Feel the sensations conveyed through your senses, such as touch, taste, smell, and sight. Be mindful of your body and its needs.

Thought observation: Learn to consciously observe your thoughts without letting them carry you away. Let them come and go without giving them any evaluation or meaning. Through this practice you develop a distance to your thoughts and can perceive more clearly what is happening in the present moment.

Slow down and enjoy: Consciously take time for everyday activities and enjoy them fully. This could be eating a meal, reading a book, or taking a walk in nature. Slow your pace and be present for each action you take.

Mindfulness in relationships: When you interact with other people, be fully with them. Listen carefully, notice their body language, and be present in communication. This fosters a deeper connection and creates space for meaningful interpersonal encounters.

Mindfulness in everyday life: Integrate mindfulness practices into your daily routine. These can be brief moments of silence and self-reflection, or deliberate actions like turning on a piece of music that inspires you before you begin a task.

The practice of mindfulness and presence allows you to experience being alone more consciously and intensely. By focusing on the present moment and sharpening your senses, you can establish a deeper connection with yourself and your surroundings. This leads to a more fulfilling and balanced life.

10.2.7 Goals and dreams

An important aspect of integrating aloneness into a fulfilling and balanced life is the focus on goals and dreams. Being alone provides an opportunity to focus on and actively pursue your own desires and ambitions. Here are some steps that can help identify and act on your goals and dreams:Reflection:Take time to think about your desires, passions and interests. Ask yourself what you really want to achieve in life and what your dreams are.

SMART goals: Set clear and specific goals that are measurable, achievable, relevant and time-bound. Formulate your goals in such a way that they motivate and challenge you, but are still realistic.

Planning: Develop a concrete plan to achieve your goals. Break them down into smaller steps and set a timeline. Also consider what resources and support you will need to achieve your goals.

Self-motivation: Keep your motivation high by regularly reminding yourself of your goals and empowering yourself with positive affirmations and visualizations. Celebrate small progress and remind yourself why your goals are important to you.

Flexibility: Be open to change and adjust your goals as necessary. Life can be unpredictable, and it's important to adapt and find new ways to achieve your dreams.

Support: Seek support from those around you. Share your goals with trusted friends or family members and ask for their support. You could also seek out a mentor or coach to guide and motivate you along the way.

Self-reflection: Take time regularly to reflect on your progress and review your goals. Ask yourself if they are still relevant and if you are on the right track. Adjust your plans as necessary to ensure you are pursuing your dreams on the best possible path.

By focusing on your goals and dreams, you can find clear direction in your life, even when you are alone. Hold yourself accountable and track your progress. Achieving your goals will not only bring a sense of fulfillment and satisfaction, but will also help you live a full and balanced life while alone.

10.3 The inspiration from stories and experiences of other loners

A valuable source of inspiration and motivation in dealing with being alone are the stories and experiences of other solitary people. Reading books, listening to podcasts, or watching movies about people who value and succeed in their alone time can offer new perspectives and ideas. Here are some ways you can benefit from the experiences of other loners:

Books and Biographies: Read books or biographies by loners who write about their experiences of being alone. These stories can offer you insights, wisdom, and practical advice on how they dealt with loneliness and lived fulfilling lives while alone.

Podcasts and Interviews: Listen to podcasts or watch interviews of loners who talk about their experiences. They often share their ups and downs, their strategies for coping with loneliness, and their insights into how they've used being alone as an opportunity for personal growth.

Online communities: Join online communities or forums where loners share their stories and experiences. Here you can learn from others, ask questions, get support, and connect with like-minded people.

Personal conversations: Seek exchange with other loners in your personal environment. Talk to friends, acquaintances or other people who have had similar experiences. Through dialogue, you can learn from each other, gain new perspectives and develop solutions together.

Social media: follow social media accounts of loners who share inspiring content. Through their posts, quotes or stories, they can encourage you to make the most of being alone and create your own journey of personal growth.

Workshops and Events: Participate in workshops, seminars or events that focus on being alone and personal development. Here you have the opportunity to learn from experts and like-minded people, gain new perspectives and get inspired.

The stories and experiences of other loners can remind us that being alone is not only challenging, but also provides a valuable opportunity for personal growth and self-discovery. Use these sources of inspiration to gain new ideas, manage your loneliness, and live a fulfilling life while alone.

10.3.1 Media recommendations

1. Books and biographies:
- "Walden" by Henry David Thoreau: a literary classic in which Thoreau reflects on his two years in a log cabin in the countryside and explores the benefits of being alone.
- "Eat, Pray, Love" by Elizabeth Gilbert: An autobiographical narrative in which Gilbert describes her journey of self-discovery and being alone through different countries.
- "The Alchemist" by Paulo Coelho: An inspiring novel about a young shepherd who embarks on a spiritual journey and discovers his personal legend.
2. Podcasts and interviews:
- "The Tim Ferriss Show": a podcast where Tim Ferriss talks to successful people about their experiences, habits and personal development.
- "SuperSoul Conversations" with Oprah Winfrey: Oprah Winfrey interviews inspiring people from various fields and talks about topics such as self-discovery, spirituality and life fulfillment.
3. Communities and forums:
- "Introvert, Dear": an online community and blog focused on the experiences and needs of introverts and loners. Here you can read stories and share with others.

- Reddit community r/Solitude: A community on the Reddit platform where people share their experiences of being alone and give advice.
4. Films and documentaries:
- "Into the Wild" (2007): A film based on a true story that portrays a young man who leaves his previous life behind and moves alone into the Alaskan wilderness to get to know himself better.
- "Jiro Dreams of Sushi" (2011): A documentary about Japanese sushi master Jiro Ono, who has dedicated his life to perfecting his craft, including spending a lot of time alone.
5. Mentors and role models:
- Mahatma Gandhi: A political leader who advocated nonviolent resistance and spiritual development. His philosophy and way of life can serve as inspiration on how to use being alone for personal transformation.
- Frida Kahlo: A Mexican artist whose painting and life story are characterized by personal strength and self-expression. Her approach to loneliness and creative development can be inspiring.

These examples are meant to give you a glimpse of what kind of books, podcasts, communities, films, and role models you can explore for your own inspiration and motivation in dealing with being alone. There are, of course, many more works and personalities for you to discover. Choose the ones that best reflect your interests and values and help shape your own journey of being alone.

10.4 The conclusion and outlook for a fulfilling future of being alone

Being alone is a valuable experience that allows us to get to know ourselves better, discover our interests and develop personally. By addressing feelings of loneliness and consciously creating alone time, we can lead fulfilling and balanced lives. Here are some closing thoughts and a glimpse of a fulfilling future of being alone:

Self-Reflection: Take time for honest self-reflection on your experience of being alone. Reflect on how you have grown, the challenges you have overcome, and the lessons you have learned. Acknowledge your strengths and accomplishments and be proud of yourself for the courage you have shown to embrace and work on your solitude.

Gratitude: Show gratitude for the people who have supported you during your journey of being alone. Think of friends, family, mentors, or professional helpers who have stood by you during difficult times and helped you overcome loneliness. Appreciate their support and recognize the importance of social connection and interpersonal relationships.

Future Plans: Create a vision for a fulfilling future of being alone. Consider how you can pursue your interests, passions, and goals. Plan activities, projects, or travel that will inspire you and further your personal development. Hold on to your dreams and set realistic goals to live a fulfilling life of being alone.

Continued Growth: Recognize that the journey of being alone is an ongoing process. Ongoing self-reflection, self-care, and personal growth are critical to getting the most out of being alone. Be open to new experiences, learn from challenges, and stay curious about what life has in store for you.

Seek support: Remind yourself that it is okay to seek support when you need it. Although being alone can be a valuable experience, it is important to recognize that there may be times when you need support, whether from friends, family members, or professional helpers. Don't hesitate to ask for help if you feel you need it.

Finally, know that being alone is an opportunity to get to know yourself better, develop personally, and live a full life. Use this time to pursue your interests, strengthen your relationships, and realize your own dreams. With a positive attitude and a willingness to make the most of being alone, you can create a happy and fulfilling future.

Manufactured by Amazon.ca
Acheson, AB